CANADIAN SPIES

— AND —

SPIES IN CANADA

Undercover at Home & Abroad

Peter Boer

FOLK LORE PUBLISHING

First printed in 2005 10 9 8 7 6 5 4 3 2 1

Printed in Canada

The Publisher: Folklore Publishing

Website: www.folklorepublishing.com

Library and Archives Canada Cataloguing in Publication

Boer, Peter, 1977–
   Canadian spies & spies in Canada : Undercover at home & abroad
   /Peter Boer.

(Great Canadian stories)
Includes bibliographical references.
ISBN 1-894864-29-8

   1. Spies—Canada—Biography. 2. Spies—Canada—
History—20th century. 3. Espionage—Canada—
History—20th century. I. Title. II. Title: Canadian spies
and spies in Canada. III. Series.

UB270.5.B63 2005   327.12′092′271   C2005-901455-5

Project Director: Faye Boer
Project Editor: Scott Rollans
Production: Trina Koscielnuk
Cover Design: Valentino

We acknowledge the support of the Alberta Foundation for the Arts for our publishing program.

PC:P6

Table of Contents

Dedication

In memory of my great grandfathers—
Henk and Cornelis

You gave your lives so I could have mine.
I will never forget.

~⚬X⚬~

Acknowledgements

No book would have been possible without the enduring support of my mother (and publisher) Faye who continues to give me every opportunity to succeed in life, or that of my father Hank and brother Ryan. My thanks also to Scott, my editor, for pointing out all the tiny mistakes, even though I often felt like kicking myself afterwards. A big thank you as well to all my friends and all my co-workers for their support during what has been a difficult time—no man can stand alone, and I am proud to have you at my side. And lastly, to my Oma and Opa, Anton and Suzanne Boer, whose fathers gave their lives in the Second World War: their memory has endured through your lives. I will always be humbled by your courage.

~⚬X⚬~

Introduction

WHEN A PERSON THINKS OF SPIES, THEY SELDOM THINK of Canada.

True, the history of espionage in Canada dims in comparison to our neighbours to the south. There have been no Canadian spies on par with Americans like Julius and Ethel Rosenberg, executed for passing on nuclear secrets to the Russians. Nor has any agent risen to such a dizzying height of power as Robert Hanssen, a senior FBI counter-intelligence agent who passed secrets to the Russians for 15 years until his arrest in 2001.

But Canadian spies have emerged, beginning in World War II and spreading out across the wide expanse of the Cold War. Some were recruited from within our country's institutions, and some infiltrated Canada from beyond its borders. This book brings together the names, places and procedures of espionage agents previously described only in scholarly works, along with some who have simply been forgotten over time. It also tells the stories of the people behind Joint Task Force Two and Camp X—two operations linked to Canada's intelligence history.

Spies represent a dichotomy. Those who spy against foreign countries are celebrated for their heroism and commitment to ideals. On the other hand, citizens who betray their own country's secrets are castigated as traitors.

Why do people spy? This book puts forward a number of reasons, ranging from sexual blackmail to ideology, from revenge to excitement. Although we

can try to boil a spy's motivations into simple cate-
gories, each one has his or her own reasons for spying.

For example, when Igor Gouzenko defected to the
West with a bundle of classified Soviet documents, it
was widely believed that he had betrayed the Soviet
Union because of his love for Canada. What emerged,
however, was more a tale of personal salvation than
political conversion. Gouzenko served overseas in a
highly sensitive position, during a time when the
slightest suspicion was cause for imprisonment or
execution. When he received word he and his wife
were being recalled to Moscow, Gouzenko decided to
roll the dice and take his chances. Though the ensuing
political fray uncovered a spy ring in the Canadian
public service that extended across the Atlantic to
Great Britain, Gouzenko spent the rest of his life
struggling to protect his reputation and enshrine himself in the public imagination.

William Stephenson's reasons for service were similar, but more noble. The Winnipeg-born businessman indebted himself to the British in the 1930s by
passing along industrial intelligence on the growing
German war machine. When Prime Minister Sir
Winston Churchill established the office of British
Security Coordination (BSC) in New York, Stephenson readily accept the post as the organization's head.
Though BSC's activities were later inflated by
pseudo-historians—most of whom worked at the
behest of Stephenson himself—Stephenson's true
accomplishments cannot be ignored. The "Man
Called Intrepid" never forgot his Canadian roots,
even though he seldom returned home.

Others engaged in espionage for more material
reasons. For some, the lure of power and money

proved irresistible. In the case of RCMP officer James Morrison, a love of the good life motivated him to betray his country and the identity of one of the Security Service's most important double agents. The yacht-sailing, well-dressed policeman sold out for $14,000.

Hugh Hambleton, a quiet, tortured soul who yearned for more attention than his career as a student of economics offered, found it as a spy for the Soviet Union. He photographed NATO documents for them, then promoted their interests in Haiti and Peru.

Some, however, had little choice in their roles as spies. Werner Alfred Waldemar von Janowski, a German agent who was dropped off on Canada's Gaspé peninsula by a German U-boat during World War II, was captured on his first day in country. He had no choice but to serve as a double agent, but records show he may have tipped off his German controllers in some of his earliest communications.

John Watkins was a distinguished scholar and diplomat. He was also a homosexual, a fact the KGB seized upon in an attempt to blackmail him during his service as ambassador to Moscow. We know the KGB approached Watkins about his indiscretions in an attempt to force his hand, but whatever secrets he may have shared died with him during his interrogation.

The best spies, however, are patriots. The ranks of both Joint Task Force Two and Camp X were filled with soldiers committed to protecting their nation. The Canadian special forces soldiers of JTF-2 have served all over the world. At Camp X, a British spy school established in Ontario during World War II, spies of many different backgrounds—American,

Canadian, British, Yugoslavian, Hungarian—all committed themselves to the defeat of Hitler's Third Reich.

It could be argued, however, that high-level spies have existed in Canada and have simply never been found. The history of the RCMP Security Service is dotted with intelligence failures. In many cases, spies were only arrested after they turned themselves in, or were exposed by informants. Perhaps future scholars will be able to unearth those facts as the government gradually loosens its grip on classified historical documents.

CHAPTER ONE

William Samuel Clouston Stephenson
aka Intrepid, aka The Quiet Canadian
(1897–1989)

SPAIN OR PORTUGAL, SOMETIME DURING WORLD WAR II

Although he noticed the men, he didn't show it.

He sat like a duck, calm and placid on the surface but thrashing away beneath. His presence in this country was not well publicized, yet these men were craning their necks around, obviously looking for someone in particular. In the world of espionage, a man was trained not to believe in coincidences.

He kept his eyes on the "toughs" and tried to make himself as inconspicuous as possible, bowing his head below the brim of his fedora. But it was too late. He spotted a glimmer of recognition in the eyes of one of the men. Using eye contact and barely perceptible hand signals, that man caught the attention of the others, and they all homed in on where William Stephenson was sitting.

But Stephenson was always prepared. He had spent enough time in the spy game to know that the only thing one could predict was the unpredictable. He stood up casually and began to back away from the men. He avoided their eyes, seemingly staring at the floor as his hand dipped into his jacket, his fingers frantically tickling his breast in an effort to extract his pen. His fingertips closed around its end just as the first of the men arrived. As he removed the pen, the others encircled him, demanding in no uncertain terms that he accompany them.

He twirled the pen in his fingers as if considering their request, until the tip was pointed away from his body. As he opened his mouth to speak, he pulled on the pen's clasp. A sharp click sounded, but no pen tip emerged. Instead, a cloud of noxious, irritating gas hissed out in a forceful blast, directly into the faces of his would-be captors. They had no time to cover their faces. The second the gas touched the mucous membranes of their eyes, noses and mouths, they began to scream and rub frantically at their faces. They stumbled into one another, falling to the ground as the world evaporated into a milky stain before their eyes.

Stephenson didn't wait around to watch. He was on the move the moment the gas billowed from his pen, stepping around the men and running into the night. He heard their screams as he flew out the door but felt no satisfaction, only relief that he had escaped.

Soon, the only trace of Intrepid was the echo of his footsteps as he disappeared into the night.

Like his career during World War II, the formative years of William Samuel Stephenson are shrouded in mystery.

Given the nature of his future work, it was perhaps necessary that his childhood be erased and reconstructed, with disparate accounts given in various biographical works. According to *A Man Called Intrepid*, the worldwide bestseller that made him a household name, Stephenson was born in Winnipeg on January 11, 1896, to a Scottish family that operated a lumber mill. His father, legend has it, died in 1901 while fighting for the British side in the Boer War. He grew up in Point Douglas district, where he attended Argyle High School, and there he became an accomplished amateur boxer. When he reached the age of enlistment, Stephenson, like many Canadians, signed up to serve in World War I.

The version of Stephenson's childhood as told in *A Man Called Intrepid* endured until the mid-1990s, when *The True Intrepid* by Bill Macdonald hit bookstores across North America. Stephenson's past, it seemed, had been a fabrication.

In truth, claimed Macdonald, Stephenson was actually born on January 23, 1897 under the birth name of William Samuel Clouston Stanger, to a couple that had immigrated to Canada from Iceland. Although William's father did die in 1901, it was from progressive muscular dystrophy. Unable to make ends meet, Bill's mother soon gave her son up for adoption to Kristin and Vigfus Stephenson, family friends.

Young Bill grew up in the Stephenson home, applying his incredible thirst for knowledge to the world around him. He played with radios, sending Morse code messages to other radio operators and ships churning the waters of Lake Ontario. He played with kites, experimented with steam and read every book he could get his hands on.

His formal education, however, was short lived. There was never an Argyle High School in Winnipeg, claimed Macdonald. Stephenson did attend an elementary school of the same name, but formally withdrew from school after grade six. He worked as a telegram delivery person in subsequent years, as well as in a local lumberyard. He became familiar with the Point Douglas neighbourhood as he scooted around on his bicycle, delivering messages to businesses and private citizens. During this period of employment, young Stephenson had his first experience with intelligence gathering.

In 1913, John Krafchenko was a dangerous man. A known bank robber and hoodlum who had already served time in prison, Krafchenko robbed a bank that December, killing the bank manager. He was on the lam for eight days, hiding out at a rooming house in Point Douglas. Young Bill Stephenson, out delivering telegrams, recognized the robber and murderer from sketches that had been printed and posted around the city. He called the authorities, and Krafchenko was subsequently arrested. Although he escaped from custody a month later, Krafchenko was rearrested, tried and hanged for murder.

If this close brush with the criminal element had any effect on young Stephenson, he never admitted it to any author, journalist or friend. Three years later, Bill joined up with the 101st Battalion of the Winnipeg Light Infantry for combat service in the Great War. By 1916, the breadth of France was criss-crossed with the trenches of Germans and Allies who had long since fought to a stalemate. The war was devouring young men the world over, and Stephenson quickly felt its desperate grasp.

Not one week into his deployment, the newly minted soldier of the Canadian Corps was wounded and gassed in France. Although invalided from the army as a result of his injuries, Stephenson found his way back into the maw of the war that had almost claimed his life. He managed to convince his superiors he could still fight, not as a foot soldier, but as a fighter pilot.

Accounts vary as to how many kills the young Canadian actually marked during his flying career, but Stephenson distinguished himself as an able pilot. He racked up at least five confirmed kills, though by some accounts he shot down as many as 27 German planes during the war.

His streak came to an ironic end in July 1918, in the final months of the war. While on patrol along the German lines, Stephenson spotted a reconnaissance plane being attacked by seven German fighters. He leapt into the fray, dispatching three of the fighters and driving the other four away, but then he lost control of his Camel and crashed behind enemy lines. He was taken prisoner and imprisoned at Holzminden. It was later rumoured that the French reconnaissance plane he had fought to save had inadvertently shot him down.

Stephenson did not stay imprisoned for long. In October, he was apparently able to escape, although no details of his break from prison have ever been revealed. One fact did trickle down through the annals of history—Stephenson did not escape empty handed. Three days later, when he worked his way back to the Allied lines, he had a German-made can opener in hand.

He had swiped the utensil from a prison kitchen. It was a kind never before seen in North America. It could smoothly remove the lid of the most stubborn can without leaving a sharp, jagged edge. Stephenson was convinced that if he could get the device home to Canada and patent it, it would launch his business career. He did patent it when he returned to Winnipeg in 1919, and it did launch his career, though not in the way he had hoped.

The Kleen Kut can opener was just one of the wares hawked by Stephenson and Charles Russell through their business enterprise, Stephenson-Russell, Ltd. The company sold home and car accessories, as well as groceries and lumber, to businesses in and around Manitoba. Although the company started off well enough, Stephenson was forced to declare bankruptcy in 1922. Rather than face the wrath of his creditors, according to *The True Intrepid*, Stephenson caught a fast ship to England and lost himself in London.

His experiences with radio during the war came in handy in Great Britain. By 1923, he was the managing director of General Radio in London, manufacturers of the first home radios. He was also credited with helping develop a process for transmitting photographs by radio waves, establishing the foundation for what would later become television.

Stephenson quickly began to build up his vast business empire in England, establishing several successful companies. He became the owner of Alpha Cement as well as Pressed Steel. He opened General Aircraft, which designed a plane that won the King's Cup in 1934. He also started up his own film company, Sound City Films. By the 1930s, Stephenson was a millionaire, pressing the flesh with such celebrities as playwright George Bernard Shaw, actress Greta Garbo and former First Lord of the Admiralty Winston Churchill.

Stephenson's success soon gave him access to an even more vital commodity in 1930s Europe—information. It was the heyday of Adolf Hitler and the Nazi party in Germany, as the diminutive Austrian moved to consolidate his power. Germany had been stripped of her military and international standing under the Treaty of Versailles and crippled by a post-war economy that reduced the Deutschmark to fireplace kindling. Germany began to circumvent the restrictions placed on her at the end of World War I, secretly building up her army, her navy and air force. By 1936, Germany was on the move again, remilitarizing the Rhineland, annexing Austria and invading Czechoslovakia. In his business travels across Europe, Stephenson soon became the trusted eyes and ears of the British establishment. He fed information about upheaval on the continent to both Desmond Morton, head of the Industrial Intelligence Centre in Great Britain, and Winston Churchill, now a sitting Member of Parliament. He reported on the manufacture of raw materials, the rearming of Germany's military and the development of the ENIGMA cipher machine. Churchill used Stephenson's information to lambaste Prime Minster Neville Chamberlain in Parliament, demanding to know why Britain was not rearming to face the German threat.

Stephenson shared Churchill's concern, so much so he even offered to assassinate the Fuehrer himself. This ingratiated him to Churchill, a man with whom he had already forged a close bond. Bill further proved his devotion to the Allied cause in November 1939, two months after Britain officially went to war, when he participated in Operation "Strike Ox," a plan to sabotage Swedish iron-ore shipments to Germany. The plan was cancelled, however, when Swedish counter-intelligence agencies caught wind of the plot. Although he had just delivered the plastic explosive needed to complete the job, Stephenson managed to escape.

When Churchill defeated Chamberlain as prime minister in May 1940, he quickly turned to his long-time associate for help with the war effort. Churchill's principal concern was the future role of the United States in the growing conflict. Norway and Denmark had fallen quickly to the German Wehrmacht, as had Holland and Belgium, with France not far behind. The U.S. had already declared its neutrality, as the people of America sent a sharp warning to President Franklin Roosevelt not to risk the lives of American boys on foreign soil.

Churchill was determined to overcome that senti-ment, and he spied an opportunity. When World War II began, the U.S. had no intelligence capability. The Office of Strategic Services (OSS) was not even a thought in the president's mind, and both Churchill and Roosevelt were concerned with potential Nazi activity in the U.S. Roosevelt saw a role for American troops in the European conflict but needed help to overcome America's isolationism.

"You know what you must do at once," Churchill told Stephenson during a dinner in May 1940. "You are to be my personal representative in the United States. I will ensure that you have the full support of all the resources at my command. I know that you will have success and the good Lord will guide your efforts as He will ours."

Churchill clapped Stephenson once on the shoul-der. "This may be our last farewell," he said omi-nously. "Au revoir and good luck."

After a secret meeting with FBI director J. Edgar Hoover, Stephenson met personally with Roosevelt in 1940. Both sides needed to tread carefully because the establishment of a British intelligence outfit on American soil was a flagrant violation of U.S. neutrality laws. British Security Coordination (BSC), as the organization would later be known, would exist outside the realm of diplomatic propriety with no official recognition by the government.

Stephenson threw himself into the job the moment he arrived in New York in June 1940. Under the official occupational title of British Passport Control Officer, he organized one of the war's largest intelligence agencies. Although it started with a handful of close friends working out of an apartment, BSC eventually grew to employ approximately 1000 staff in two floors at Rockefeller Center in Manhattan. Stephenson's first success in his new position came when he persuaded the U.S. to send an emissary to Great Britain to assess England's war capability—"Wild Bill" Donovan, a Republican lawyer whom Stephenson had originally met during World War I.

It was a stark time for the once-mighty nation. The evacuation of British troops from Dunkirk, France, though seen as a success, left thousands of artillery pieces, tanks and rifles in German hands. Hitler was already looking north, across the English Channel, hoping to launch Operation "Sealion"—the invasion of Great Britain—by September 1940. In his report to Roosevelt, Donovan underscored how poorly equipped England was. As a result, the U.S. agreed to lease 50 retired destroyers to the Royal Navy for convoy duty, as well as one million rifles and100 Flying Fortress bombers.

With Great Britain's war materiel demands temporarily satisfied, Stephenson turned his mind to America. He recruited hundreds of Canadian women to work as secretaries, because U.S. citizens were not allowed to work for the BSC. He established contacts within local foreign language schools and cultural groups, looking for sources of information on Axis activity in America. His agents began to monitor German nationals living in the United States and to tail "suspect" sailors on ships docking in New York. BSC also recruited journalists and writers to help overcome America's mounting isolationism. Reporters attacked pacifists as Nazi sympathizers, along with isolationist groups like "America First." Stephenson even authorized BSC to subsidize a New York radio station WRUL as a propaganda vehicle.

To keep tabs on German interests in North America, BSC, in conjunction with British embassies in the Caribbean, began an aggressive mail-reading strategy. BSC opened letters routed through Bermuda, on their way from North America to Europe. They scanned each letter for the locations of persons of interest in the United States, as well as for information that spies might be trying to send overseas. Readers also combed each package for signs of secret writing in invisible inks or microdots (photographs of documents, reduced to the size of periods or commas). Although the mail-reading operation violated fundamental principles of democracy, over the course of the war, BSC staff gleaned a great deal of information from the letters and intercepted several microdots and invisible-ink messages.

Letters believed to be from foreign intelligence operatives were passed onto the FBI for follow-up.

One of those letters, however, quickly revealed BSC's growing role in U.S. counter-espionage. The letter mentioned the unfortunate death of a man named "Phil," who had been hit by a taxi and then run over by a second car while crossing a street in New York in March 1941. According to *A Man Called Intrepid*, Hoover confronted BSC about the letter. Stephenson admitted that Phil, also known as Ulrich von der Osten (a known captain in the German Abwehr) had been "removed" deliberately.

Similar stories also came to light after World War II. *A Man Called Intrepid* describes the blatant assassination of a Japanese consular employee by BSC. The Japanese consulate, prior to the attack on Pearl Harbor, was located directly below the BSC offices in Rockefeller Center. The staff at BSC eventually discovered that one of the cipher clerks was intercepting their messages. One night in the summer of 1941, a team of BSC agents set themselves up in a skyscraper directly facing Rockefeller Center. When the cipher clerk came into view, a sharpshooter—rumoured to be Ian Fleming, the creator of James Bond—shot him in the head.

Stories of assassinations and "removals" were never substantiated beyond what was written in *A Man Called Intrepid*, but the BSC had many equally hair-raising exploits during the war. Elizabeth Pack, code-named "Cynthia," was one of BSC's most successful agents. An attractive American with a voice that could melt ice, Cynthia had helped evacuate civilians during the Spanish Civil War. Later, she seduced an aide in the Polish Foreign Ministry and convinced him to hand over secret documents. When Cynthia was brought back to the United States, Stephenson set her up in Washington and unleashed her on the embassies of both the Italian government and the Vichy French.

Although few in North America knew it, in 1942, the Vichy French were little more than a lapdog of the Nazis, set up to govern the south and west portions of France. It was Cynthia's job to expose the Vichy for what they really were.

Again, Cynthia did not disappoint. Posing as a journalist, she established a relationship with the press attaché at the Vichy embassy, Charles Brousse. As the two grew closer, Brousse began to confess his frustration with the Vichy regime. When the time was right, Cynthia told Brousse of her true mission and asked if he would be willing to help. He did, passing along many secret documents from the embassy. But Stephenson was after the big fish from the Vichy French—naval ciphers that were kept in a locked safe inside the embassy.

This formidable challenge did not deter Cynthia. With Brousse squarely in her pocket, she set to work planning the operation. She and Brousse spent an entire week inside the embassy, engaging in "undercover operations" to desensitize the guards to their late-night presence. One evening, the two sneaked a Canadian safecracker into the embassy, and he quickly figured out the combination to the safe. A few nights later, Cynthia and Brousse returned and began removing the ciphers from the safe. At one point during the night, when Cynthia heard an embassy guard making his way down the hall, she quickly removed her clothing and threw herself upon Brousse.

"Je m'excuse!" the guard exclaimed when he saw the naked couple writhing passionately on the couch in the office. Brousse waved the man away, and the pair opened the safe and removed the ciphers. Within 20 hours, the codebooks had been photographed by BSC operatives, and returned to the safe undetected. The information gleaned from the daring operation led to the roundup of all Vichy embassy officials, including Brousse. When Brousse was released after the war, he and Cynthia moved to France together and were married.

The scope of BSC's operations gradually expanded into other parts of the world. The Nazis were trying to export their philosophy to the poverty-stricken countries of South America. British embassies throughout the area intercepted wireless traffic and forwarded it to BSC in New York. Stephenson and his senior staff began to sow discord between the German emissaries and their host governments in an effort to combat the growing Nazi presence in Latin America.

In May 1941, Stephenson worried that the Nazis were planning a coup in Bolivia. BSC operatives forged a letter from Major Elias Belmonte of the Bolivian Legation in Germany to the German Minister in Bolivia. The letter spoke of "liberating" Bolivia from its current government and said that a supreme leader of all South America would eventually be required. It took two of BSC's best operatives to adequately forge Belmonte's signature. The letter was placed in the Bolivian diplomatic pouch and then "stolen" by another BSC agent in Buenos Aires. When the Bolivian President saw the letter, the German minister was expelled from the country, the German embassy was closed and all Nazi sympathizers were arrested.

Such forgeries, in Stephenson's view, were a necessary evil of war. "Nothing," he is quoted as saying, "deceives like a document." The Bolivian incident was not the first occasion in which the BSC used subterfuge to achieve its goals overseas. A second letter forged by BSC in the name of the President of LAITI, the Italian commercial air service, hinted at a Nazi-inspired plot against Brazilian president Getulio Vargas. When Vargas was informed of the contents of the letter, he immediately revoked LAITI's landing rights. Brazil, which had hung precariously between Axis and Allied allegiances, moved into the Anglo-American sphere of influence.

American citizens had already been involved in the war on a clandestine level for years. In 1940, Stephenson, in conjunction with the Canadian, American and British governments, established Camp X (Special Training School 103) on a farm outside Whitby, Ontario. The camp was designed to train American and foreign combatants in the secret arts of sabotage and clandestine warfare behind enemy lines in Europe. Students learned the intricacies of unarmed and armed combat, explosives and booby-traps, ciphers and codes, as well as escape and evasion techniques. Camp X's "Station M" produced fake documents for agents headed overseas, and with the HYDRA array— a series of radio transmitters—established a secure radio link between Ottawa, Washington and London.

Over the course of the war, Stephenson became known as "God" to his staff of approximately 1000. He was a speed-reader with a photographic memory, able to scan and absorb voluminous reports in mere minutes. He seldom left the office, reclining in his desk chair up to 20 hours a day, poring through countless sheaves of documents.

His position and power, though questioned frequently by American statesmen and even Hoover himself, proved invaluable to the U.S. In 1941, when Roosevelt ordered the establishment of the OSS under the directorship of "Wild Bill" Donovan, Stephenson helped his American friend set up the new intelligence agency. "Bill Stephenson taught us all we knew about foreign intelligence," Donovan later said.

Stephenson also drew on BSC's vast resources to conduct operations behind enemy lines in Nazi-occupied Europe. He was able to secure the use of three torpedo boats in 1942 to help extricate Danish atomic scientist Niels Bohr from Sweden. Bohr had been living under Nazi rule since Denmark had first fallen in 1940, oblivious to the fact that the Germans might want to use him to help develop an atomic bomb. In 1942, when the Nazis overthrew King Christian X and began a harsh repression of the Danish people, Bohr fled to Sweden. Eventually, he was transported to England in the belly of a plywood Mosquito bomber.

The war took a personal toll on Stephenson. Besides the long hours and stressful nature of the job, "Intrepid" often used his own personal fortune to subsidize the operating expenses of BSC. He drew no salary during his tenure as the head of the organization and often put himself at risk. He virtually dropped off the face of the planet, seldom contacting family or friends in Winnipeg. Although he apparently visited Manitoba once following the war, he never bothered to look in on any relatives. When his mother died in 1940, Stephenson did not attend the funeral nor send any message of any kind. He never had a child of his own, so devoted was he to the war effort.

That devotion, however, was effectively sealed from the public when the war ended in 1945. The moment the news of Japanese surrender reached the ears of the American public, BSC began to pack its boxes. With the war over and the OSS up and running, the agency was no longer needed. A history of BSC was written in secret, and 10 copies were locked away in a safe. In 1946, the bulk of the agency's records were taken by truck to Camp X and destroyed.

Stephenson was called on one last time in September 1945, when Igor Gouzenko, a nervous, young cipher clerk working in the Soviet Embassy defected to Canada. Stephenson lobbied the authorities to accept Gouzenko and his information, even sending two of his most senior staff to Canada to help the RCMP debrief the Russian clerk.

By 1946, however, the "Quiet Canadian" (as he came to be known) was effectively finished in the spy game. He returned to the world of business in the 1950s, living in New York and becoming honorary chairman of Manitoba's Economic Advisory Board. In the early 1960s, however, the dauntless Intrepid suffered a severe stroke that left him in need of constant nursing care. He and Mary moved to Bermuda, where Stephenson lived out his last 20 years. He stayed in touch with the world through his teletype, receiving messages from world leaders and officials and occasionally being asked for advice.

When Montgomery Hyde (whose travel expenses had been paid for by Stephenson) published *The Quiet Canadian* in 1962, the name of "Little Bill" Stephenson finally became known to the rest of the world. That mystique heightened when William Stevenson (no relation) penned *A Man Called Intrepid* in 1976.

As Stephenson's renown grew worldwide, so too did international efforts to properly honour his wartime achievements. In 1980, after years of lobbying by Canadian journalists and BSC alumni, Governor General Edward Schreyer finally awarded Stephenson the Order of Canada. Three years later, U.S. President Ronald Regan named Stephenson the recipient of the William J. Donovan Medal.

The two awards came almost 40 years after Stephenson had first been knighted in England. "This one," Churchill had written in the column of Stephenson's citation, "is close to my heart."

In 1989, at the age of 92, William Stephenson passed away at his Bermuda home. At his request, news of his death was withheld from the press until after his body was buried.

CHAPTER TWO

Werner Alfred
Waldermar von Janowski
(1904–1978)

AS THE MORNING SUN BROKE OVER THE GASPÉ PENINSULA, Werner Alfred Waldemar von Janowski began to stir.

It was not quite yet 7:00 AM on November 9, 1942. Janowski was happy to see the first few tendrils of light snake their way across the sky. Light brought relief and warmth to the cold, damp cove in which he had spent the evening.

His Kriegsmarine uniform was soaked through from the late night and early morning chill. He was hungry and tired, and he was sure he smelled like 40 unwashed men. His hands were scraped and cut from trying to climb out of the cove several hours before.

Emerging from cover, Janowski stretched mightily and then approached the near-vertical cliff that separated him from the highway above. In the growing light, his eyes picked out a path that he hadn't seen when he had first tried scaling the cove shortly after midnight. He picked up his two briefcases and began to mount the craggy bluff.

It was slow going. The cases, one of which contained his Afu radio transmitter, were awkward. He stopped every few minutes to listen for the sounds of traffic above, but heard nothing. After what felt like hours of climbing, he was able to throw one briefcase up over the ledge and use his free hand to pull himself up. He peeked over the ledge, watching and listening. Still no one.

Moving swiftly and surely, Janowski mounted the bluff and skittered into a nearby thatch of trees for cover. He stripped off his uniform and donned a civilian pair of slacks, a shirt and a trench coat. Still looking over his shoulder, he chose a suitable spot and, with a shovel given him by the crew of U-518, quickly dug a shallow hole. He threw the uniform into the hole, heaping dirt back over it.

All he could hear was the gentle crash of the Atlantic Ocean on the coast of the Gaspé Peninsula. The highway snaked ahead of him, beckoning him into a foreign country. For just a moment, Janowski felt desperately lost and alone.

Grabbing both briefcases, the German spy turned and walked off down the road, and into an unknown fate.

All heads turned as the stranger stepped into the Carlisle Hotel in the town of New Carlisle, Québec. He was pale and unshaven and carried two briefcases. A truck had dropped him off in front of the hotel minutes earlier. He asked for a dayroom—just so he could take a bath—and some breakfast. The clerk at the till breathed through her mouth as a sour, briny smell washed over her. She handed him the key to Room 11, where he could find a bath, then directed him to the kitchen.

Earle Annett Jr., the son of the owner, peered at the man as he mounted the stairs to his room. There was something out of place about him, something that tickled at Earle's mind. His jacket, Earle noted, was unlike any fashion he had seen locally. And Earle's nose picked up the man's scent.

When the stranger came back downstairs to the kitchen later that morning, his smell had changed little. Although he looked much more refreshed than when he first arrived, his clothes remained saturated with the unmistakable odour of the sea. The man again approached the clerk, still carrying his briefcases.

"How much for cigarettes?" he asked in a guttural, unfamiliar accent. He then pulled a dollar bill from his jacket and handed it to the clerk to cover the cost of his room and the smokes.

It was Canadian currency, of that the clerk was sure, but a bill that had not been printed in Canada since 1935. It was notably larger than the standard dollar bill now printed by the Canadian mint.

"Is there something wrong?" He asked the clerk.

"No, just this kind of money hasn't been in circulation for a while," the clerk responded, cashing the bill anyway.

"Ah," the man said cautiously. "I am from Sweden," he offered by way of explanation. He then grabbed his briefcases again and strode into the dining room, where he ordered breakfast.

While the man ate, the clerk passed the bill to Earle Annett Sr., owner of the Carlisle Hotel. Between that and the clerk's story about how the visitor had not known the price of a pack of cigarettes, Earle Sr.'s curiosity was aroused. He approached the man in the dining room and began chatting with him, at first innocently, then more directly.

"Did you come in on the bus from Chandler?" Earle Sr. asked.

"Yes, from Chandler," the man responded brusquely between bites of food.

Earle Sr.'s spine tingled with excitement and fear. The bus to Chandler had been cancelled months ago. It was all adding up in his mind...the smell, the cigarettes, the dollar bill and now this. *Maybe he was a spy!*

Earle Jr., standing behind his father, was thinking exactly the same thing. When the man finished his breakfast and asked when the next train to Matapedia left the station, Earle Jr. noticed something on the ground. A matchbox had fallen from the man's coat. Perhaps another clue.

Suddenly, the man stood, grabbing his suitcases and ran out the door. It happened so suddenly, the Annetts sat a moment in shock. Earle lunged for the matches. The box, which stated the matches were made in Belgium, lacked an excise stamp, required on all imported products.

Now they had something. The Annetts acted fast. Earle Jr. hopped in the family's Chevy truck and roared to the train station, where he found the stranger sitting back having a cup of coffee. When the man boarded the train, Earl noted where he sat, then alerted the train's naval policeman, Johnny Lozinsky. But Lozinsky was reluctant to act, because such matters fell out of his jurisdiction. Instead, the two hopped in the Chevy and sped to the local Québec Provincial Police detachment.

There, they explained the situation to Constable Alphonse Dascheneau. Although he viewed their story with some skepticism, Dascheneau decided to accompany Annett and Lozinsky back to the train station.

As soon as Dascheneau boarded the train, he confronted the man directly, demanding to see his papers. The stranger produced a Canadian Nation Registration Certificate in the name of William Branton, along with a Québec driver's license that showed a home address in Toronto. Warning bells sounding in his head, Dascheneau demanded that the man open his two suitcases . With nowhere to run, his fragile story already in tatters, the man bowed his head and sighed.

"I am caught," Werner Alfred Waldemar von Janowski said. "I am a spy."

The train had already left the station. Fortunately for Dascheneau, the next stop was at Bonaventure, where one of his men waited.

During the journey, Janowski told the assembled spy-catching party that he was a naval officer who had come ashore from a U-boat off the Canadian coast. His mission was to search out targets for future attacks. The submarine, he said, would be returning for him in a few days.

Janowski asked to be allowed to dig up and don the navy uniform he had buried earlier that morning, and Dascheneau agreed. The police officers then took Janowski to a nearby hotel, placed him under guard and began to make phone calls.

Word spread like a wildfire across Québec and Ontario, as well as into the United States. The heads of the QPP, the RCMP and the various branches of the armed forces were alerted to the spy's capture. Officers from the QPP, RCMP and Naval Intelligence were dispatched to New Carlisle to interrogate the prisoner.

The townspeople were atwitter with the news of the capture, and word soon began to trickle outside the confines of the tiny town. Police detachments along the Atlantic coast beefed up their patrols, and two minesweepers were ordered into the Bay of Fundy to look for the submarine that had delivered the spy. The FBI and the British Security Coordination in New York were alerted, and border patrols between the U.S. and Canada were stepped up. U.S. journalists, tipped off by police sources, began calling their Canadian counterparts, demanding answers. At first, press censors stepped in, refusing to allow any Canadian news agency to broadcast reports of the capture.

On November 11, after a 600-mile drive, Cliff "Slim" Harvison of the RCMP arrived in New Carlisle to take control of the prisoner. Harvison was a Montréal detective who had made his career pounding the pavement and tracking down drug dealers and users. He was by no means a counter-intelligence operative, but RCMP Commissioner Stuart Wood ordered him to interrogate the prisoner. On the return drive to Montréal, Janowski found himself sandwiched between Corporal Joseph Bordelau and a former intelligence operative codenamed "Johnny" who spoke fluent German. Not long into the drive, Janowski cracked.

He began his story during the drive and continued once they reached the RCMP headquarters on Sherbrooke Street. Janowski claimed to be a reluctant spy, who had been bullied into taking the mission after making some decidedly un-Nazi comments during a drinking binge with fellow officers. He had also been selected for the mission because he had lived in Canada during the late 1920s and early 1930s. He had even been married, he said, to a successful hat maker named Olive Quance. He had served with the French Foreign Legion for five years, and upon discharge, had been imprisoned by the Nazis until being recruited into the army, where he had served in Holland, Belgium and France.

Harvison was convinced that Janowski was telling the truth. He instantly began evaluating the situation for the potential of performing one of the espionage game's trickiest manoeuvres—the double-cross. Perfected by the British, the double-cross involved "turning" a spy without letting the enemy know. His captors would use him to feed false information back to his home agency and solicit important intelligence in kind.

Harvison had Janowski's radio, his codebooks, as well as two matches whose heads were actually made of an invisible writing material called quinine. During the interrogation, Janowski had shared other vital elements of his contact orders, including his radio frequency, broadcast times and a letter grouping Janowski was to insert into every message to identify himself. The potential to learn about espionage networks and other saboteurs who may have come ashore in North America was, Harvison felt, too great to ignore. He recommended that the double-cross proceed, and Wood approved the order.

Unfortunately, Janowski's anonymity quickly became threatened as a series of news stories found their way past the news censors and were released in the United States. In the days immediately following Janowski's arrest, a newspaper in Memphis published a short story on the capture of a spy who came ashore, and a radio station reportedly broadcast a similar story two days later. On November 19, a small article in *Newsweek* also mentioned Janowski's landing, though it didn't reveal his name. Harvison believed the stories didn't compromise Janowski's position, and he decided to proceed with the double-cross operation.

Janowski's first job was to send a letter to his superiors, addressed to a post office box in Sweden. In large, block letters, he wrote a fake letter requesting payment of an overdue account. Then, using one of his special matches, he wrote an invisible message alerting his Abwehr controllers that he had landed safely.

Days later a Naval Intelligence officer approached his superiors in alarm. The letter and envelope in which it was mailed had been copied on photostat and filed away. An officer reviewing the file pointed out that, when spelling his cover name of "Dr. I. H. Nauckhoff," Janowski had written the "I" to appear more like a "J." He had also misspelled the name of the street to which the letter was posted. Either error, the officer argued, could be a tip-off to the Abwehr that Janowski had been captured and turned.

Those warnings were ignored. The next phase of the plan—making contact by radio—began without delay. Janowski was due to report to his controlling officers in Hamburg by radio by December 1. The RCMP found a house on the outskirts of Montréal that could be used inconspicuously to transmit messages. They also recruited Gordon Southam, an amateur radioman, to try to learn Janowski's "fist" (his personal style in sending Morse code) should Southam ever need to fill in for him. An experienced radioman on the other end could recognize a person simply by the way in which he sent his dots and dashes.

According to Janowski, he was to check in with Hamburg at 4:30 AM and 6:30 PM, Central European Time. Any message sent over the Afu set would be coded using one of two novels Janowski had brought with him—*Mary Poppins* and a collection of detective stories. Janowski chose letters from prearranged pages and scrambled the original message, then alerted Hamburg as to which book he was using as code. Corporal Ken Molyneaux of the RCMP had the task of learning the code and double-checking all of Janowski's transmissions to ensure he did not slip in any hidden warnings to his Abwehr masters.

The first month of transmissions passed without success. Although Janowski could at times hear the faint beeping of the Hamburg station over the headset of his Afu, they never responded to any of his messages. Southam even built a small booster for the radio, powerful enough to increase the strength of the Afu's transmissions, but gentle enough not to rouse the suspicions of anyone listening on the other end.

A few more weeks passed with no response. Harvison became so nervous that, on December 21, he asked Janowski to write another letter to the mail drop in Sweden. This one, scrutinized more carefully by Molyneaux, contained no deliberate misspellings.

On January 5, 1943, the RCMP moved Janowski and his radio unit to the basement of a house in the

borough of Mount Royal. They set up small anten-
nae in the back yard to allow Janowski to transmit
over the "noise" of Montreal more easily, but he still
got no answer.

Finally, on January 14, an operator in Hamburg
made contact. The message told Janowski to switch
his contact time to 3:30 PM and to stay off the air until
February 1.

Harvison, however, was no longer alone in running
the double-agent operation. The RCMP had forwarded
a copy of his preliminary report to MI5, England's
vaunted counter-intelligence agency. The report had
been so amateurish and so full of holes, the agency felt
obliged to send one of its own representatives to
Canada to help with the plot.

"The papers from Montréal gave us more of a laugh
than a comic paper. They made a monkey of Harvison," one former MI5 employee later said.

The man chosen for duty was Cyril Mills, a hard-
headed, intelligent man who successfully managed
several different double agents over the course of
World War II. Mills was a no-nonsense hard-ass with
a distinguished record at MI5. The first thing Mills did
was give the entire affair a codename—"Watchdog."

Mills brought all of his skill to bear on Janowski. He
was convinced the spy was still lying to the RCMP
about his origins. When he met the German, Mills
looked him straight in they eye and told him to 'fess
up or he would be hanged. This new, stricter approach,
coupled with the fact Harvison was away for a month
preparing for a trial, weakened Janowski's resolve. By
the time he resumed communications with Hamburg,
he had changed his life story for a third and final time.

He confessed that he was a long-time member of the Nazi party and had served in both the Frei Korps Schmidt and Black Reichswher in the 1920s. Both of these groups had worked to secretly build up the German armed forces in defiance of the Treaty of Versailles that had ended World War I. He had also been a pilot and flight instructor for the Luftwaffe. Yet, in 1930, he had boarded a steamer bound for Canada. For nearly a year, he prowled around southern Ontario, looking for work as a farm labourer. Then he met Quance, dismissed in mainstream society as a 44-year-old well-to-do spinster. He wooed her, charmed her into marriage and spent most of the next two years spending her money. He took radio classes and did some work as a radio repairman. In 1933, he legally changed his last name to "Brampton."

In 1933, he abruptly told Quance that he was leaving her to join the French Foreign Legion, and he served in North Africa for five years. Upon his discharge in 1938, he was imprisoned at a German concentration camp until his father managed to negotiate his release. In exchange, Janowski was recruited into the Abwehr as a saboteur.

He was first deployed to Morocco, where he had served with the French Foreign Legion, and put to work running guns and explosives to Arab subversives in the area. He did so well, he was promoted. On the eve of the invasion of Holland in 1940, Janowski and a group of 50 men penetrated the tiny country ahead of the main invasion force, trying to prevent a key bridge from being destroyed.

Janowski later saw work in Libya, where he was stationed with Erwin Rommel's Afrika Corps, and in Belgium and France, where he mercilessly hunted down Allied spies. He also remarried, this time to a German woman whose family owned a toiletries factory. Despite his record, Janowski continued to maintain that he had been forced into his current assignment because of the anti-Nazi remarks he had made at a drinking party.

With the air cleared, Janowski got to work on the Afu set in the basement of the Mount Royal home. The RCMP had begun assembling information, most of it public knowledge, and fed it to Janowski, who passed it on to his masters in Hamburg. He sent information about the quantity of Canadian rations, the location of air force training schools as well as inflated statistics on the production of aircraft, rubber, tanks and steel. His handlers also allowed him to insert small greetings to his wife and family back home.

But the efficacy of the Watchdog operation was quickly becoming debatable. There had been more breaches of censorship; for example, a prominent Québec politician mentioned Janowski's arrest during a public speech, and the press picked up his remarks. Janowski's controllers in Germany were also acting fairly tamely, acknowledging receipt of the second letter he had sent, but not the first. Although they occasionally asked him for specific information, they often simply passed along well wishes from his wife.

Janowski had originally told Harvison and Mills that more agents were due to land in Canada during the coming spring. As spring approached, however, Hamburg sent no instructions to Janowski about helping these new agents. In early May, when Janowski advised Hamburg (in a message composed by Harvison) that he had located several sympathetic German workers in Montréal factories, his superiors responded that he was to "work at all costs alone." When Mills found out about the message later, he objected to it. Harvison had focused on making a few busts locally, but Mills had hoped to use Janowski to mislead the Germans about the location of the imminent Allied assault across the English Channel.

After a month of sparring, Harvison and Mills finally decided to transmit a message asking Hamburg whether or not any "helpers" would be landing ashore soon. Janowski received a response the next day, but with no mention of any helpers. The message simply said, "Thanks and greetings from home. All is well here. Bruno." Even Janowski was visibly perturbed. The message seemed too crafted, too scripted to be from anyone but his superiors.

Meanwhile, news stories continued to slip past the war censors. On June 14, a newspaper in Halifax ran another article on Janowski's arrest. Wood feared that Janowski's cover had long since been blown. With the approach of autumn, it was obvious there was no longer enough time left in the season for the Germans to land any "helpers."

On August 11, Operation Watchdog was shut down for good. The decision proved wise. Mills had left for a brief trip back to England, and had left a stack of blank code sheets for Janowski to fill in. When he returned to Canada and reviewed the transmissions, he discovered Janowski had deliberately misspelled one message in an attempt to convey the word "SOS."

Mills suspected that Janowski had not been operating as a double agent, but as a triple. Besides the code sheets, there had been the misspellings in the first letter to the Swedish mail drop and the repeated messages to his family. Perhaps Janowski was even *supposed* to be caught, to distract Allied attention from other operations. The Abwehr may have deliberately given him the oversized dollar bills to speed up, if not ensure, his capture.

Janowski was sent to Britain, and after a final debriefing, MI5 imprisoned him until 1947. When he returned to Germany, he discovered that the army had not issued any of his required pay. In 1948, Janowski contacted Wood, asking for a letter confirming that he had, in fact, been serving as a German spy overseas during the war. Wood dutifully replied.

In 1963, while travelling to Germany as the new commissioner of the RCMP, Harvison received a phone call from Janowski, suggesting a meeting. But the next day, the former spy sent a telegram saying he could not make it.

Janowski died in Germany in 1978. The uniform he wore when he came ashore, as well as the radio, his gun and many of the other odds and ends found in his suitcase were stored by the RCMP and were eventually unveiled in a museum in Saskatchewan. They stand as a silent tribute to Canada's first and ultimately futile foray into the world of intelligence in World War II.

CHAPTER THREE

Canada's Secret Spy School

APRIL 20, 1943

When the red light turned amber, Stevan Serdar stood up.

The cabin of the Halifax bomber had been frightfully cold on the flight from Cairo. Stevan had spent the entire flight sitting on the hard bench, leaning back against his parachute and trying not to count the minutes until he and his two companions jumped.

The drone of the bomber's four engines was intermittently accompanied by the bang and crackle of flak exploding around the aircraft. With no windows, all Serdar could do was stare at the floor and try not to imagine what would happen if a round struck the aircraft. He tried to focus on the mission, mentally reviewing the instructions he'd been given and thinking back to the training he'd received several months earlier at the strange farm in Ontario, Canada.

Now that the amber light was on, Serdar's mind switched to automatic. The former Quebec miner and veteran of the Spanish Civil War stepped forward as the bomb bay doors parted inches from his feet. It was like staring into a bottomless, black ocean. Serdar braced himself against the wind that rushed into the cabin.

The jumpmaster yelled out a warning, and Serdar heard his two companions fall into line behind him. The light changed again, this time from amber to green. Without a thought, Serdar stepped out of the plane and into the inky blackness below.

His free fall was short. His parachute sprang open with a rustle of silk, and the harness dug painfully into his armpits. He looked around and saw the other two members of his team floating lazily in the air above him. They hung in the air for what seemed like an eternity, completely exposed to German guns. Finally, the ground rushed up to meet them, and Serdar landed with a thump in his native country of Yugoslavia.

He rolled with the impact and quickly gathered his parachute. He heard his two squad mates land nearby, then the rumble of war in the distance. He checked the pocket of his jumpsuit and was relieved to find his side arm still in its holster.

They buried their parachutes, shed their jumpsuits and began to move out. Serdar took a bearing with his compass, as he had been taught in Canada, and found his location on a map. They were close to where they were supposed to be, but the Germans were also nearby. Serdar motioned to the two men under his command, and together they started to make their way silently across the Bosnian countryside, towards their rendezvous with Tito's partisan fighters.

I'm a long way from Camp X, thought Serdar, *but, still, it's good to be home.*

The thunderous explosion shattered windows in Oshawa, over four miles away.

The broken windows were a nuisance, but they weren't really a surprise. By now, the locals had learned to ignore the repeated booms of demolition work, the buzz of low-flying aircraft and the security patrols that stopped any vehicle that got too close to the abandoned farm at Whitby. According to the military, the base was used to test explosives.

But the personnel at Special Training School 103 (STS-103)—later dubbed Camp X—didn't test explosives. They tested men. The spy school had been dreamed up in September 1941, on a New York rooftop. World War II was raging throughout Europe, but so far, the American people had no interest in fighting overseas. Perhaps a Canadian spy school could entice the Americans into the war.

Great Britain had already established the office of British Security Coordination (BSC) under the directorship of William Stephenson, a Canadian. From his office in Rockefeller Center, Stephenson worked with his staff to turn the tide of public opinion against the Germans and to gather intelligence on Axis activity in North America. At the beginning of the war, the United States lacked an intelligence organization, save for an army signals unit. Roosevelt had made it privately known that he wanted to intervene in Europe, but that the time just wasn't right.

On the night September 6, 1941, Stephenson met with British and Canadian representatives for a rooftop dinner at his apartment. They decided that night that BSC would construct a secret training unit—a spy school—to prepare American spies for their eventual involvement in the war effort. Because the Americans were officially neutral, the school could not be built in the United States. It also wasn't safe or feasible to ship American intelligence recruits across the Atlantic to any of Britain's Special Operations Executive (SOE) schools. Stephenson suggested building a new school in southern Ontario.

The construction followed quickly. Within a week, Vancouver businessman Alfred James Taylor, a friend of Stephenson's, had arranged the purchase of 260 acres of farmland on the north shore of Lake Ontario for $12,000. The site was close enough to Whitby and Oshawa to allow for convenient recreation and resupply, yet far enough away to maintain secrecy. It offered a wide variety of terrain: flat expanses, forests, swampland, and rocky bluffs along the lakeshore. In short, it would provide an ideal training ground for the future spies of World War II.

On December 6, 1941, exactly three months after Stephenson's rooftop meeting, the first staff began to arrive at Camp X. The next day, the Japanese fleet bombed Pearl Harbor and the U.S. declared war.

The staff at Camp X did their best to teach recruits as much as possible. In the SOE hierarchy, however, STS 103 was more a kindergarten than a finishing school. Most students spent no more than two months at the camp, and few could gain the skill needed for spying and subversion in such a short time. Successful graduates from Camp X moved on to more advanced schools in Britain.

A typical day at Camp X began with an early breakfast in the mess, followed by a 10-hour day of lectures, physical training, combat practice and night exercises. Recruits lived in individual rooms and had access to an extensive library of books on espionage, both fiction and non-fiction. But the training process began before the recruits even set foot in camp. Americans arriving in Toronto by train were given specific instructions and a code phrase. Every recruit had to successfully locate his contact and use the correct phrase before he would be taken to Camp X.

Camp X specialized in preparing agents for operations in Axis-held territory. Personal protection and silent killing were among the most important drills. Students were taught to disarm, maim and kill with their feet, fingers and elbows.

The instructor in silent killing, Captain William Fairbairn, was among the first Europeans ever to receive a black belt in jiu-jitsu. The 57-year-old firebrand had honed his fighting skills in the 1920s as a member of the municipal police in Shanghai. He showed his students how to kill a man with a single blow, how to break an enemy's neck and dislocate his spine. The key point, Fairbairn stressed to his students, was never to give the enemy a chance to fight back. "Even if you think you have already subdued him," he urged, "kick him in the testicles."

Students also trained extensively in the use of firearms. "Ignore the sights on your weapons," their teachers advised. "Just point your gun toward the target, and keep pulling the trigger until he goes down." Every agent spent at least one hour each night on the firing range, handling as many different kinds of weapons as possible—from revolvers to tommy guns.

In one of the most intense drills, the trainees stood behind panes of bulletproof glass while instructors fired live ammunition at them. That way, they would not be overwhelmed with anxiety while trading shots with the enemy. Students also tackled a variety of obstacle courses while instructors fired over their heads to create as realistic a combat environment as possible.

The live ammunition exercises were not without casualties. In May 1942, barely a month after he had joined the staff, Major Howard Burgess was struck in the head by a stray round while showing students how to crawl under a barbed-wire fence. Though he clung to life for five days, Burgess ultimately succumbed to his wounds.

Instructors routinely roused students in the middle of the night, drove them out to a secluded field and left them with only a compass and a map to a specific location. When an agent successfully reached his objective, he was often driven to yet another location and told to find his way home.

Operatives were taught how to move silently through fields and thick foliage and to shield themselves from the glare of the moon and the exposure of a ridgeline. They were thrown into Lake Ontario from the top of a 30-foot bluff and then ordered to climb up the rocky face without a rope.

Those who would be organizing sabotage missions behind German lines were schooled in the proper use of explosives. They learned how to use both dynamite and plastic explosives to destroy buildings, bridges, roads and rail lines. Sometimes, though, they couldn't resist testing their skills on more mundane targets. On one occasion, a nearby stream became jammed with ice, and two students decided to dislodge the dam with six sticks of dynamite. The ensuing blast shattered windows in Oshawa and showered ice, mud and rocks onto Camp X.

The students were also sent on mock missions to industrial sites in the area. STS-103 had been built near a General Motors plant and an ammunition factory run by Defence Industries Limited. Watchmen at both sites would be warned on a particular day to be on the lookout for suspicious activity. Students would try to penetrate the plants' security, recover documents or lay phoney explosive charges and then escape undetected. Engineers on the trains that passed through the north end of the camp sometimes spotted young men crouched in the bushes beside the railroad tracks, trying to stay out of sight as they pretended to sabotage the rail line.

When they weren't in the field practicing orienteering skills or blowing up abandoned vehicles, the students attended courses in the camp's lecture hall. Lieutenant-Colonel Bill Brooker, who ran Camp X for most of the war, taught his students the basics of disguise, escape and evasion, as well as how to recruit spies behind enemy lines. An agent could alter his appearance by dying his skin darker, cutting his hair or putting newspaper in his shoes to make himself taller.

Students developed false identities, or "legends," and practiced using them as often as possible. They were taught to guard against inconsistencies between their legends and their behaviour, to wear certain clothes, eat certain foods and smoke in a particular way. "Once you're in the field, the tiniest slip-up could cost you your freedom or even your life," Brooker warned. The secret to success, he said, was repetition. "The more times you tell a lie, the more likely you are to come to believe it."

In the first months, most of the recruits who passed through Camp X were Americans sent by the Office of Strategic Services (OSS). By the summer of 1942, however, the OSS had lured several instructors, including Fairbairn, to its own training camp in Maryland, nicknamed "the Farm." Now that the U.S. was a full participant in the war, fewer Americans attended Camp X. More and more, Brooker travelled to the U.S. to give weekend presentations to instructors and potential agents.

The camp's outlook changed in other ways as well. The Nazis had begun planning to penetrate and even overthrow unstable governments in Latin America. Already, BSC had launched operations against the Germans in Brazil and Bolivia, but the Allies feared that several other countries, including Argentina, could give safe haven to German U-boats operating in the Atlantic. With few agents in the field in Latin America, the British also began to fear for the security of many large British-owned industries with operations in South America. To counter the threat, the British began sending Latin-speaking personnel to Camp X, to train for security duty in South America.

Camp X also began recruiting amateur radio operators for deployment to South America. Although most ham radio operators had been ordered to shut down for the duration of the war for security reasons, British MI6 officer Eric Curwain began actively recruiting them. He needed people to monitor the airwaves for communications between agents in Latin America and the German broadcast station in Hamburg. Curwain's recruits were put through special training at Camp X with particular emphasis on codes and ciphers. Once they were deployed in South America, they were to monitor one or several radio frequencies for suspicious activities.

Eric Adams was among the Canadian ham radio operators recruited and trained at Camp X. Deployed to Santiago, Chile, Adams remained awake throughout the night, copying down the dots and dashes of Morse code and forwarding them to BSC for analysis. During 1942, Adams monitored a frequency that MI6 believed was being used by a group of Argentinean generals to plan a coup. One day, however, the signal disappeared without warning and never returned.

Camp X also played an important role in the world of communications. Once the Americans had entered the war, the U.S. and Canada needed to share information and intelligence as quickly as possible. The Germans, however, knew of the existing phone and teletype lines. Instead, the two countries established a secure communications facility at Camp X to trade information between London, Ottawa, New York and Washington. Codenamed HYDRA, the communications facility boasted three different antenna arrays, ranging in power from 2500 watts to 10 kilowatts. Construction on the first antenna began shortly after Camp X opened its doors in December 1941. Three SOE agents scoured North America for parts, then shipped them to the camp along with a photograph showing what the assembled antenna should look like.

"Have at her, boys," one of the officers offered by way of instruction when all of the parts arrived.

Eventually, HYDRA became one of the most important communications links between Great Britain and North America. Information received from London was recorded as a series of dots and dashes on paper tape, and then rebroadcast over a secure landline to New York or Washington and vice versa. Benjamin deForest Bayly, head of communications at BSC, invented an online cipher machine to handle the sheer volume of information passing through the HYDRA array. He nicknamed it the "Rockex," in honour of Radio City Music Hall's famous dancing showgirl troupe, the Rockettes.

By the midpoint of the war, Camp X was training special squads of immigrant Canadians, for missions to their home countries overseas. In 1942, SOE requested the RCMP track down 100 Canadians of Yugoslavian descent for potential service behind enemy lines. Hitler had invaded Yugoslavia in April 1941, but the Wehrmacht was encountering stiff resistance from several groups in both Croatia and Bosnia. The SOE, in its efforts to support the resistance movement, decided to train Yugoslavian immigrants to parachute behind enemy lines and work as liaison officers.

The RCMP recruited approximately 40 Canadians, many of them illegal immigrants or communists, and sent them to Camp X for training. In April 1943, six trainees parachuted into Yugoslavia. Three linked up with resistance forces in Bosnia, and the other three sought out Marshal Tito's Croatian Peasants Party. The six operatives, all of them fierce patriots, organized supply drops and communications between Allied forces and the resistance movements. Nickel Kimball, a Vancouver lumberjack who had trained at Camp X, parachuted into Bosnia, Serbia and Macedonia on three separate occasions to work with resistance forces in Yugoslavia. Of those Yugoslavians who trained at Camp X, five were killed by the Germans.

Among the most important agents trained at Camp X, however, was a group of French Canadians who played a crucial role in the invasion of Normandy in June 1944. Operation Overlord, in planning since 1942, sought to establish an Allied land presence on the continent through an invasion of the French coast from across the English Channel. When D-Day came on June 6, 1944, 300,000 Allied troops stormed five different beaches on the Normandy coast and successfully established a foothold in Europe.

Part of the Allied success on D-Day was due to the work of undercover agents who worked behind German lines to disrupt Wehrmacht units trying to reach the front. Several were French Canadians who had been trained at Camp X.

Jean-Paul Archambault had been serving in the Canadian Army Postal Corps when he was selected for training at Camp X in 1943. Parachuted into France prior to the invasion, Archambault contacted several SOE "circuits," or French resistance networks, and trained them in the art of sabotage. When D-Day came, Archambault and his resistance fighters successfully delayed German reinforcements by blowing up railroad tracks in and around Lyons. He was later joined by a second French-Canadian who had also trained at Camp X, Guy D'Artois.

Sadly, Archambault's heroic exploits came to an end in 1945 on the island of Burma. He had been picking his way through the Burmese jungle with a sack full of plastic explosives looking for Japanese troops to ambush. One day, while trying to dry out some of the explosives, he was badly injured in a blast. He lived for several days after the incident, chronicling his misfortune in a diary before dying from his wounds.

Leonard Taschereau had been working in an aircraft plant when he volunteered for duty at Camp X in 1943. The Saskatoon native parachuted into France one week after D-Day and linked up with another French resistance circuit operating in Troyes. Taschereau put his fighters to work harassing the Germans, organizing late-night raids on German formations and sabotaging roads, railways and bridges.

Joseph Benoit was remembered by his friends as a "dark, decisive man with a poker face and a remarkable skill at card games." Those assets came in handy when Benoit, then in his 30s, was parachuted into France two weeks before D-Day. In the short time Benoit spent in France, he created the most havoc. He twice cut a German telegraph line using sulphuric acid, and blew up several ammunition and fuel dumps behind German enemy lines. He was also among the first agents to locate one of the German's V-1 rocket launch sites. The "buzz bombs" launched from the French coast had been pummelling Great Britain, buzzing through the sky and then dropping with a terrorizing wail when they ran out of fuel. After Benoit located the launch site, the RAF "bombed the hell out of it."

By the time Operation Overlord was underway, Camp X's utility had come to an end. Both the OSS and SOE already had plenty of agents harassing the retreating German army and gathering intelligence. In April

1944, SOE ordered the closure of STS-103, which had trained 500 agents in its two-year existence.

Despite the departure of SOE, Camp X continued to operate well into the 1960s. In 1945, William Stephenson ordered all of BSC's documents shipped from New York to the camp so that a detailed history of the organization's history could be prepared. The book, written in total secrecy and considered classified to this day, was completed in a matter of months. Twenty copies were printed, and then all of BSC's documents were destroyed.

Later, in September 1945, a young GRU cipher clerk named Igor Gouzenko walked out of the Soviet embassy in Ottawa with a jacket full of confidential papers, exposing a Soviet spy ring in Canada. The RCMP sheltered the frightened young clerk and his family at the old farmhouse at Camp X while agents from Great Britain, Canada and the United States debriefed him. Their RCMP keepers did their best to make the Gouzenkos feel at home at Camp X, going all out that December to give them a real Canadian Christmas. The mood of the occasion was spoiled, however, when the Gouzenkos' young son went onto the roof and urinated into the stovepipe, basting the turkey in an unhealthy manner.

Canadian military personnel continued to operate HYDRA until the 1960s, though their activities are still considered classified. They most likely used the three arrays to listen in on Soviet transmissions during the height of the Cold War, but the government has never acknowledged it. By the end of the decade, HYDRA was deactivated, and Camp X faded into the history books.

Despite repeated attempts to create a museum dedicated to the site's important role in World War II, all that remains of STS-103 today are a few ramshackle buildings and a plaque dedicated to the memory of those who trained and served there.

CHAPTER FOUR

Igor Gouzenko
(1919–1982)

He was Russian, Chester Frowde was sure of that.

Frowde, the night editor for the *Ottawa Journal*, was in the paper's morgue, where back issues of the paper were kept for reference. Across from him stood a small, dishevelled man, eyes wide with fear, stumbling over what few words of English he seemed to be able to speak.

Since entering the building, the man had spoken little. His accent was thick, most definitely Russian. He would try to speak, then stand silently. He was sweating profusely, his blonde hair ragged. He seemed to carry a crushing secret, but couldn't spit it out.

Then there were his clothes. Underneath his jacket and shirt, bundles of papers bulged against the seams, their white corners peeking from the collar of his jacket. Every time the man shifted, his clothing rustled with paper on paper.

Frowde ran a hand through his hair, trying to pick the right words.

"Sir," he said. "I'm sorry, but I don't know how I can help you."

The man's eyes bulged again, and he breathed in sharply, nervously. He blinked, then, in a sudden jerk, shoved a hand up under his jacket. There was the crunch of paper and when he pulled his tight, shaking fist out, it clutched a sheaf of documents.

The man thrust the papers at Frowde. He took them and looked them over. Some were on white paper, others on blue. From what he could see, almost all of the documents were written in Cyrillic characters, the alphabet of the Russian language. Frowde flipped through them one after another. They looked important, but he couldn't tell what they were.

He had just opened his mouth to ask another question when the man suddenly spoke. His voice echoed through the morgue with a dreadful pronouncement.

"It's war." The man said. "It's Russia."

Igor Gouzenko had only seen one orange in his life when he arrived in Canada.

It was June 1943, and the 24-year-old Russian was on a layover in Edmonton, Alberta, waiting for the train that would take him on the final leg of his journey to Ottawa. He was a cipher clerk, a lieutenant in the *Glavnoye Razvedyvatelnoye Upravleniye* (GRU), the military intelligence branch of the Red Army of the Soviet Union. Having completed an uncomfortable journey over the Atlantic Ocean by plane, he and several of his comrades were on their way to a new posting at the Soviet Embassy. During his wait, as he explored the area around the train station, he stumbled across a grocery store. His eyes popped at the sheer quantity of fresh fruit, and he quickly stocked up on oranges, spending the remainder of his travel allowance. He feasted on them throughout the train trip to Ottawa, haphazardly discarding the peels, laughing as oranges spilled from their crate and rolled along the aisles of the passenger car.

There was little such luxury or freedom in the Union of Soviet Socialist Republics. The monarchy that had ruled Russia had been overthrown by a democratic revolt in 1917. That movement was then toppled by a group of communists, known as the Bolsheviks, led by the enigmatic Vladimir Ilych Lenin. Lenin believed in Marxism, a political philosophy that railed against the free market system that had begun to industrialize much of the world. All of human history and conflict, according to the philosopher Karl Marx, could be analyzed in the context of an ongoing struggle between the upper and lower classes of society, the *bourgeoisie* and the *proletariat*. Lenin was determined to lead a workers revolt against the *bourgeoisie*, eliminate class distinctions and allow the state to provide for the needs of everyone.

Before his death in 1924, Lenin established the USSR and conquered the forces of the old monarchy that sought to overthrow him in a bloody civil war. His successor, a short, moustached Georgian named Josef Stalin, quickly consolidated his power with a heavy hand. He purged the armed forces and Communist Party of anyone he believed opposed his rule. He used the state's secret police, the *Narodny Komissaryat Vnutrennikh Del* (NKVD) to arrest and execute citizens thought to be disloyal. The slightest suspicion of opposition to Stalin's rule was grounds for either execution or exile to one of the dreaded labour camps, known as *gulags*.

Naturally, those working in intelligence faced particular scrutiny. The Red Army selected Gouzenko following his graduation from the Academy of Engineering in Moscow, but he had to wait several months before starting work, while the NKVD conducted background checks. Once his loyalty was sufficiently proven, Gouzenko was trained to code and decode Soviet military and diplomatic communiqués. As a cipher clerk, he was entrusted with the knowledge of current USSR codes and procedures. He was given a fake name and personal history, then dispatched to Ottawa to work in the embassy.

At that time, in 1943, there was no Cold War. The USSR, United States, Great Britain and Canada were all allies, working to stop the advances of the German military throughout Europe in World War II. The armed forces of the Soviet Union were struggling to repel the German Wehrmacht from the borders of the Motherland. The fighting was fierce, especially in and around the cities of Leningrad and Stalingrad, as Soviet conscripts battled German soldiers in a war of attrition. The Allies of the west provided planes, guns and other war materiel to bolster the Soviet campaign, which, so far, had suffered horrific losses. Despite the supposedly friendly relations between Canada and the USSR, the Soviet Union began using its newly established embassy in Ottawa to weave a web of spies throughout the nation's capital. Both the GRU and NKVD cultivated their own sources within the Communist Party of Canada, the Canadian Armed Forces and the public service. Gouzenko worked in Room 12 of the embassy, coding reports from Soviet agents for broadcast back to Moscow and decoding orders from the government to its embassy agents. Because his work was deemed to be so sensitive, he could, at any time, deny access to his workroom to any other officer posted to the embassy.

Although members of the diplomatic corps were urged to shun the trappings of capitalism and a free society, Gouzenko slowly began to love his life in Canada. He lived in a small apartment not far from the embassy with his wife Svetlana, who had joined him with their son shortly after his arrival. They often spent time together at the local grocery store, perusing the treasure-trove of items available for purchase. Even in a country that was rationing its food and supplies to fuel the war effort, Gouzenko and "Anna" found much more available to them than they could even dream of back home.

Freedom of speech and of the press also left an indelible mark on the Gouzenkos. Newspapers, even during wartime, frequently published harsh criticisms of government policies. People on the street openly questioned the actions of the government—something that, in Russia, would result in a visit by the NKVD in the middle of the night. But what really impressed Gouzenko was the national election of June 1945. He read and listened as candidates attacked one another's policies in an attempt to win the vote of the people. Such openness did not exist back home. Consequently, when Igor Gouzenko learned that same summer that he was to return to the Soviet Union, he began to despair. Stalin was still as paranoid as ever, continually purging the diplomatic corps of suspected traitors or dissidents. Most diplomatic personnel who were recalled simply disappeared after returning home. Their fate, though never publicized, did not require a great leap in imagination. Not only was he at risk, so too was his family. Anna was his best friend and the love of his life, and she was now pregnant with their second child. If they returned and Gouzenko was killed or sent to the gulag, Anna could very well follow. Their children would be taken from them and sent who knows where. Igor quickly came to the realization that returning home was not an option. He needed to keep his family safe. He needed to defect.

As the cipher clerk at the embassy, Gouzenko had access to important details about the activities of the NKVD and GRU in Canada. So far, the Canadian government had no inkling of what the embassy staff was up to. If Gouzenko could convince the right people of what was happening, maybe he could buy his freedom, not with money, but with information.

He also knew he would have to be careful. If his supervisors sensed even the slightest hint of disloyalty, they would not hesitate to act. So, as Gouzenko awaited word of his return date to the USSR, he slowly began to gather information. He marked the most important documents that crossed his desk by folding over one corner so that, when the time came, he would be able to rapidly identify them. He and Anna discussed the matter repeatedly, leaving their apartment and walking in the park for fear their home had been bugged by the NKVD. She supported him fully in his decision. She had no desire to return to the USSR.

In late August, the Gouzenkos finally received word: they were to return home within the next month. They could delay no longer. Igor and Anna finalized their plan to defect, and on September 5, 1945, Gouzenko made his move.

He went about his tasks at the embassy, as he did every day, but kept his eyes riveted on the clock in Room 12. When the rest of the staff began to leave for the day, Gouzenko reached into the canvas sack and removed 109 documents that he had marked over the last few weeks. With no briefcase and no other way of carrying them, he stuffed all of the documents underneath his shirt and walked out of the Soviet embassy for the last time.

While it may have seemed natural for Gouzenko to head straight to the nearest RCMP detachment, he was suspicious of the police based on his experience with the NKVD back home. He also thought there might be Soviet spies within the country's police organization. Instead, he made for the office of the *Ottawa Journal*, one of the capital's leading daily newspapers.

The night staff at the *Journal*, however, was less than receptive to his attempts at communicating. A reporter working the desk took one look at the small, dishevelled man who spoke poor English and passed him off to the night editor, Chester Frowde. Although Frowde tried his best to understand what the tiny Russian man was trying to tell him, Gouzenko's anxiety and fear short-circuited his command of the English language.

When Gouzenko finally managed to blurt out, "It's war. It's Russia." Frowde at first didn't believe him. "I think I...told him we're not at war with Russia and don't expect a war with Russia," Frowde later said. "Our relationship with them was apparently quite normal."

Not realizing he was passing up what would have been the biggest news story since the end of World

War II, Frowde led Gouzenko to the elevator and suggested he take his case to either the RCMP or the Department of Justice. Gouzenko didn't object; everything was happening too quickly for him to process.

His first plan hadn't worked. The journalists he had thought were the defenders of freedom didn't welcome him with open arms . Instead, he walked into the elevator and back into the street, all the while examining the people around him for familiar or suspicious faces.

When he finally arrived at the Department of Justice, it was well past 9:00 PM. Much to his despair, the office was closed for the day. A commissionaire patrolling the building told him to come back in the morning. There was nothing Gouzenko could do. He went home.

There he quietly told Anna of the difficulties he had experienced trying to defect. They spent a nervous, sleepless night in their apartment, and then set out with their son the next morning to the Department of Justice. This time, Gouzenko was able to speak to a receptionist and present his documents to the staff. He demanded a personal meeting with justice minister Louis St. Laurent but was rebuked. The mass of classified, stolen information put the office staff into a panic. Eventually, one of them told Gouzenko simply to return to the Soviet Embassy and put the documents back where they belonged.

The Gouzenkos were dumbfounded. They had thought the government would eagerly accept their defection and information. Now they were not sure what to do. Still wary of turning himself into the police, and knowing the fate that would befall him if he returned to the embassy, Gouzenko decided to try the newsroom at the *Journal* one last time.

If Frowde had been skeptical of Gouzenko's story, the day staff was even more so. This time, however, Gouzenko managed to summon enough self-control to tell the entire story to reporter Elizabeth Fraser. Fraser was stunned at the enormity of the tale and equally suspicious of its veracity. She took the story to Chuck Milne, the day editor, who told her to send the Gouzenkos away.

"I told him this was not a story the newspaper could print under present circumstances," Fraser later remembered. "It would have to be authenticated through the government. We had just finished the war, but we were still very much in the ambience of controlled news."

Despite Gouzenko's desperation, Fraser refused to hear his pleas. She took him to the windows of the newsroom and pointed to the Supreme Court building, several blocks away. She told him if his family became naturalized Canadians, the Russians would not be able to touch them.

Rebuked a third time, their situation deteriorating with every hour that Gouzenko spent away from the embassy, Anna and Igor marched into the Crown Attorney's office and demanded to apply for citizenship.

A receptionist at the office, Fernande Coulson, informed the Gouzenkos that they did not qualify for citizenship. Finally, Gouzenko unloaded his story on the unsuspecting secretary. He told her of his position in the embassy, of the documents he had taken and of his intention to defect. Unlike the others who had heard the story before, Coulson believed him.

Unbeknownst to the Gouzenkos, however, the Canadian government was already aware of his activities. Undersecretary of Justice Herbert Norman had been at the Department of Justice building that morning when Igor and Anna had been turned away by the staff. Norman had informed Prime Minister Mackenzie King of the affair, but King, in his usual fashion, was reluctant to act. In fact, in his diaries, which were later made public, King hinted that the country might be best served if Gouzenko simply killed himself.

Consequently, when Coulson phoned King's private secretary Sam Gobeil and told him what was going on, Gobeil told Coulson to "have nothing more to say or do with that man. Get rid of him as soon as you can." Coulson, however, could not turn her back on Gouzenko. She phoned the *Journal* to verify Gouzenko's story, then managed to arrange an appointment with the inspector of the RCMP for the next morning. It was now after 5:00 PM, and the Gouzenkos were forced to return home for another long night's wait.

Gouzenko was certain that by this time the Russians would be suspicious of his absence. He had now missed a full day of work without reporting to his superiors. The Russians might have also noticed that documents were missing. They would do everything in their power to make sure none of those secrets were turned over to the West.

The Gouzenkos sat quietly in their apartment, waiting for morning. Suddenly someone began to pound on the door, shouting Igor's name. Igor and Anna sat in the bedroom, trying to be as quiet as possible, the air in the apartment thick with fear. Suddenly, their son

Andrei got up and tottered away. Anna lunged for him and put a hand over his mouth. Through the thin walls of the apartment, they heard one of their neighbours inform whoever was knocking that the Gouzenkos were not home. They heard the sound of retreating footsteps. Gouzenko looked out the window and saw two men sitting in a car, watching the apartment.

If they stayed in their apartment, Gouzenko realized, they would surely be caught. Once he was sure the man who had been banging on the door had left, Igor went to see his next-door neighbours, Harold and Mildred Main. He explained their predicament and Harold, a former RCAF corporal, hopped on his bicycle to alert the Ottawa police. The neighbours across the hall, the Elliotts, offered the Gouzenkos refuge in their apartment for the evening. Only Anna managed to fall asleep on the foldout bed in the Elliotts' living room. Igor lay on the bed, staring at the ceiling, wondering what he would do.

There was a sudden burst of commotion in the hallway, the stampede of many feet quickly mounting the stairs. They heard voices, a pounding across the hallway, then the crack of wood bending and breaking. Anna and Igor, taking turns peering through the keyhole, watched as four men burst into their vacant apartment. Igor felt his breath catch in his throat. He put a finger to his lips, signalling everyone to remain silent.

Within moments, they heard more commotion. Much to the Gouzenkos' relief, a uniformed officer, Constable John McCulloch of the Ottawa City Police, approached the apartment and began to question the four Russian men. When they revealed they were from the embassy, McCulloch had little choice but to let them go, as they had diplomatic immunity. Once they left, McCulloch examined the Gouzenkos' empty apartment, then knocked on the doors of the other residents to take statements and try to locate the missing family.

On a larger scale, however, the fate of Igor Gouzenko was quickly unfolding. The government was now fully aware of what was going on and was seeking advice from larger players in the espionage field. Herbert Norman had been scheduled to dine that evening with William Stephenson, "The Man Called Intrepid," the head of British Security Coordination in New York and a major figure in the espionage world. When Stephenson called Norman to verify their plans, Norman told him about what had been happening. They immediately cancelled their dinner plans and headed for the apartment building. Stephenson recognized that Gouzenko's defection would be a major intelligence coup. He urged Norman to ignore the Prime Minister's order and place Gouzenko under protection.

The police quickly bundled the Gouzenkos out of the apartment block and took them to a motel in Ottawa. The location, however, had not been secured, and a team of RCMP officers was ordered to take them to a secure location until the following day. They drove for hours, Igor's paranoia bubbling over at the sight of every vehicle, and eventually arrived at a cottage outside Kemptville. They spent a long, anxious night there, the police bodyguards alternating shifts. The next morning, the entire party headed back into Ottawa. Gouzenko was passed off to a second detail, then taken to a cottage near Otter Lake for debriefing.

The information Gouzenko disclosed to the authorities, supported by the documents he had smuggled out of the embassy, painted a stark picture of Soviet espionage in Canada. The GRU had established a sophisticated network of approximately 20 spies in Canada, infiltrating the civil service, the military, even the government itself. Those spies were shipping information to Moscow on weaponry, nuclear technology and Allied espionage and counter-espionage efforts. No one in the Canadian government or espionage community could have predicted such a scenario.

Gouzenko's news was not just bad for Canada, but for her Allies as well. Information gleaned from Gouzenko and his documents pointed to spies in both Great Britain and the United States. He informed British authorities of spies operating within the nation's atomic weapons research division, such as scientist Allan Nunn May who was later arrested and tried, as well as the potential existence of a mole inside MI5, the country's counter-intelligence agency. Gouzenko also theorized that a very senior member of the U.S. state department was passing information to the USSR.

Keeping this source of information alive and safe became a matter of utmost concern. Gouzenko was convinced the Soviets would attempt to assassinate him if they discovered his location. Consequently, just weeks after being moved to Otter Lake, the Gouzenko family was moved to the still-secret Camp X, a farm in Ontario where the Canadian government had trained foreign intelligence operatives during the war.

During Gouzenko's stay at Camp X, RCMP officers visited repeatedly, as did intelligence officials from both the U.S. and Great Britain. Based on the evidence Gouzenko gave, the RCMP began surveillance on many of the men and women he had named. At the beginning of February 1946, an American radio journalist, who had been tipped off to the goings-on of the Gouzenko affair, broadcast the existence of the Soviet spy ring. The next day, Prime Minister Mackenzie King gave a public statement to the press, announcing the establishment of a royal commission to investigate Gouzenko's allegations.

Over the course of seven days, the commission took testimony from a total of 48 witnesses, including Gouzenko and several of the people he accused of being spies. After a total of 44 sittings, Justices Taschereau and Kellock informed Mackenzie King they believed there was enough evidence to compel the arrest of several individuals. On the morning of February 15, a synchronized team of RCMP officers descended on the homes of 18 people and arrested them for espionage activities against the government of Canada.

The list of those accused was both varied and, in some instances, shocking. Some of the arrests were obvious, such as Sam Carr, leader of the Communist Party of Canada. Others were more surprising, including army officer Samuel Sol Burman; Bank of Canada employee Agatha Chapman; Dr. Raymond Boyer, an explosives expert with the National Research Council; and Emma Woikin, a code clerk with the Department of External Affairs. The most complicated arrest was that of Fred Rose, a Member of Parliament for the

Communist Party of Canada. The RCMP had been apprehensive about arresting Rose, worried the MP could barricade himself inside the House of Commons behind the curtain of parliamentary privilege. In the end, however, they arrested Rose without incident later that spring.

The trials took more than three years, and the results were often startling. Between 1946 and 1949, all 18 of those arrested were tried but only 11 were convicted, including Rose and Carr. The penalties for those convicted ranged from two to ten years of imprisonment, but the failure to secure a higher number of convictions frustrated the RCMP. Most often, suspects who simply chose not to answer questions during the Royal Commission of 1946 were not convicted of their charges. The entire affair had shed light on a critical weak point in Canada's national security. After the Gouzenko affair, the government began to more seriously scrutinize its employees for immoral or questionable behaviour.

As for Gouzenko, he and his family did not exactly live out their remaining years in obscurity. Although he was provided with a new identity and home, as well as a modest government pension for his services, Gouzenko quickly proved to be an irritant to the government and policing authorities. He bought a farm in Ontario and began to rack up tens of thousands of dollars in debt, at one point relying on the services of a lawyer to consolidate and repay $153,000. He granted interviews to any media organization willing to pay and sold his memoirs to a Canadian publisher for a sizeable advance. He built on this success, winning the 1954 Governor General's Award for fiction for a novel entitled *The Fall of a Titan*. Although he negotiated a lucrative film contract for the book, the production company never did pick up its option.

Despite his public persona, the Canadian public never learned Gouzenko's true physical identity. Although he appeared on CBC's *Front Page Challenge* in the 1960s (for $1000), he appeared on camera wearing a white pillowcase over his head. The combination of the pillowcase, his thick Russian accent and the CBC technician's attempts to disguise his voice made much of the interview unintelligible to the listening audience.

When Gouzenko wasn't working on a new book, evading creditors or suggesting articles to journalists across the country, he was suing journalists who he felt had besmirched his name. In 1959, Gouzenko's lawyers launched a million-dollar lawsuit against Harlequin for the Frank Rasky book *Gay Canadian Rogues*, in which Gouzenko was described. Although both sides eventually settled the suit for $10,000, Gouzenko's lawyers succeeded in having the book removed from store shelves. In 1964, Gouzenko sued both *Newsweek* and *Maclean's*. Then, in 1965, he sued both the *Telegram* and the *Globe and Mail*. Although a jury in the *Maclean's* suit awarded him the grand sum of $1.00, the magazine eventually settled for $7500 when Gouzenko appealed the decision. By the time he got around to the *Newsweek* lawsuit, too much time had passed to successfully prosecute the case. Instead, Gouzenko sued the lawyer who had advised him to pursue the *Maclean's* suit instead of *Newsweek*. He lost.

Gouzenko's litigious nature continued into the 1970s, but he took a break in 1968 to try to derail the political career of Pierre Elliott Trudeau, passing out a leaflet that called Trudeau "the new Castro." When the *Toronto Star* wrote an editorial slamming Gouzenko's tactics, Gouzenko sued the paper. Again, he lost.

By 1973, however, Gouzenko was beginning to succumb to old age and disease. Diagnosed with diabetes and wary of insulin injections by unknown doctors who he feared may be trying to poison him, Gouzenko lost his eyesight. When officers from MI5 came to Canada to discuss Gouzenko's earlier testimony that there had been a mole in the British counter-intelligence agency, Gouzenko was not able to see the photos they showed him.

There were a couple of more failed lawsuits against authors, including one against June Callwood for her descriptions of him in her books *Portrait of Canada* and *Wilderness of Mirrors*. On June 25, 1982, exactly 39 years to the day since he had come to Canada, Igor Gouzenko stood in the living room of his home, listening to classical music on the radio, smiling benevolently, swaying his arms to the music as he pretended to conduct an orchestra. His joyous expression was suddenly pierced by a grimace when his heart stopped beating. Although an ambulance responded, he was already dead by the time he was taken to hospital. His funeral was a small affair, held under his assumed name, but some of those who knew him as Gouzenko managed to come and pay their respects.

Both the service and burial were brief, despite the impact Gouzenko had on the world. Although he was a thorn in the sides of both his home and adopted countries, Gouzenko has gone down in history as "the man who started the Cold War."

CHAPTER FIVE

Long Knife
(1919–??)

A PAIR OF HEADLIGHTS SPLIT THE DARKNESS ON A DESERTED country road near Aylmer, Ontario.

A handsome 39-year-old man drove the Buick a few hundred metres down the road and stopped. His passenger, a small, forgettable, pot-bellied man turned to the driver and withdrew a small envelope from his coat pocket.

"There should be about $5000 inside," he said in a slightly accented voice.

The driver nodded and pocketed the envelope. He placed his hands back on the steering wheel and stared out into the inky darkness. The world around him was almost silent. No one ever used this old road anymore. Apart from the stars, he couldn't see even a glimmer of light.

I can't believe it's come to this, he thought.

The pot-bellied man looked at him expectantly, waiting for him to speak. The driver chewed his lip, struck again by the enormity of what he was about to do. He had wrestled with his conscience since he had first approached Nikolai Ostrovsky at the Grand Hotel pub the previous day. But in the end, his need for money outweighed any patriotic or humanitarian concerns. His job was on the line and he had a valuable commodity that he could sell to the Russians—information.

"Well?" Ostrovsky asked, hands crossed over his belly.

Corporal James Morrison of the RCMP Security Service took a deep breath and began to talk.

❧◆❧

The man who arrived in Halifax in November1952 was not who he claimed to be.

The voyage across the Atlantic Ocean had been uneventful, save for Yevgeni Vladimirovich Brik's imagination. Every hour on board exhausted him as he worked to maintain the outward appearance of an ordinary person. He kept to himself, befriended no one and managed only a few hours of sleep here and there. His nerves surged when the ship docked in Halifax and he, along with several other dozen passengers, shuffled towards immigration.

The officer on duty took Brik's passport, scrutinized it, then stamped the booklet and handed it back.

"Good luck in Canada, Mr. Gladysh," he said. Brik took the passport and walked to the train station. On the trip to Montréal, he sat near the back of the train and bowed his head, speaking to no one. He closed his eyes as if sleeping, but his mind whirled. He was in a foreign country under an assumed name, separated from his wife for Lord knows how long, working under the KGB's thumb.

When the train pulled into Montreal, Brik headed to the men's room. He looked for a chalk mark on the door of one of the toilet stalls and entered. He listened for a moment, then, when he was sure he was alone, lifted the lid to the toilet tank. Taped to the underside was a bundle of papers, which he sifted through quickly. They included a birth certificate and several other documents in the name of David Semyonovich Soboloff.

He tucked the bundle into his jacket pocket, and pulled out the Gladysh passport. He tore it into shreds, flushed the scraps of paper down the toilet and headed out into the city of Montréal.

◆

James Morrison was not your typical cop.

Most members of the RCMP Security Service wore uniforms or civilian clothes, but the nature of Morrison's position meant he had to dress well—and he didn't believe in doing things halfway.

No, Jim Morrison lived on a higher level than the rest of the members of the Security Service. He always came to work in double-breasted suits, with his hair parted impeccably down the middle. He spoke perfect French, with the speed and timing of a native Québecois.

He needed a car for his job, working in the ultra-secret surveillance unit that kept tabs on suspected intelligence agents operating out of the Soviet Embassy. He drove a shiny new Buick, while most of the other agents drove nondescript older vehicles. He spent his weekends with his wife, yachting at his father-in-law's club. Everything he did, he tried to do better and richer than anyone else he knew.

So far, Jim Morrison had lucked out in life. He joined the RCMP just before the beginning of World War II and served in the Provost Corps, the army detachment of RCMP officers sent overseas to fight Hitler's armies. Although he started off as a corporal, he rose to the rank of captain by the time he was discharged in 1946. His policing career suffered a minor setback during his service in Manitoba and Saskatchewan when his rank was downgraded to corporal. But his ability had stuck in the mind of his old Provost Corps commander, now RCMP Assistant Commissioner, Len Nicholson. In 1950, Nicholson summoned Morrison to Ottawa and offered to transfer him to the Security Service, the intelligence and counter-intelligence arm of the RCMP.

When the transfer eventually took effect, Morrison's new duties were classified. He was instructed to rendezvous with Security Service Superintendent George McClellan at a park directly behind the Centre Block of Parliament. There, Mclellan gave him his new orders. Morrison would be part of a three-man unit responsible for tailing suspected Soviet intelligence officers. The men would operate out of a separate office, spending as little time as possible at the main RCMP headquarters in order to maintain their anonymity. He was to dress in civilian clothes and never refer to himself as a member of the RCMP.

The position appealed to Morrison's vanity, and he threw himself into it with gusto. The surveillance unit, however, proved less than effective. Unbeknownst to them, the three members of the squad were quickly identified by Russian agents trained in counter-surveillance. Within days, Morrison had been "made" by his subject, Ottawa *rezident* Leonid Abramov. Abramov could lose Morrison in less than five minutes anytime he needed to.

Slowly, the rules of work relaxed, and Morrison began to spend more time at headquarters. The head of the Security Service, Jimmy Lemieux, often used Morrison as his personal errand boy, to pick up his kids, his dry-cleaning or complete other tasks.

One day, Lemieux summoned Morrison to his office and told him he had a special errand for him to run. An "asset" needed to be driven from Ottawa back to his home in Montréal. Morrison was the only body available for the two-hour drive.

Lemieux should have stopped there. He didn't have to say anything more and, in the end, it would have been better if he hadn't. But Lemieux sat Morrison down and began to tell him all about the asset—the Security Service double agent named "Gideon."

❦

It did not take long for Brik to begin doubting his mission.

Shortly after his arrival in Montréal, the illegal Soviet agent started working toward his goal—to establish enough of a history in Canada that he could eventually immigrate to the United States. He went first to Toronto to familiarize himself with the city, because the real David Soboloff had lived there before returning the USSR in the 1930s. He then headed to Vancouver on instructions from Moscow. But during his travels, something happened to Brik that threw his mission off. Brik fell in love.

Unfortunately, the object of his affection lived in Kingston, a four-hour drive from Montréal. Not only that, she was married to a soldier who served in the Canadian Forces. Despite repeated proposals, he could not convince her to leave her husband and move to Montréal. The two saw one another occasionally, but the relationship was torturous for the Russian spy. It added an emotional load to an already heavy burden.

The KGB had been working him hard. Brik informed his superiors that a move to the United States would have to wait, to give "David Soboloff" a chance to file a Canadian tax return. The KGB agreed and promptly upgraded Brik's responsibilities by making him an illegal *rezident*, in charge of gathering information from intelligence agents in Canada. He received his instructions from Moscow via coded messages sent over short-wave radio, then gathered reports from agents at drop sites across the city and, in some cases, the country.

Meanwhile, Brik was also maintaining a full-time job as a photographer in order to establish a cover. The demands of his double life were proving too much for Brik. He frequently missed assignments, later claiming he had not received the messages. He seldom slept, and he lived in constant fear of being discovered. Brik's commitment was being put to the test, and it was a test he was consistently failing.

He finally reached the breaking point on a trip to Ottawa in November 1953, at a meeting with the new embassy *rezident*. Vladimir Bourdine was not known for coddling his agents. He promptly demanded to know why Brik was falling behind in his work, why he was missing so many messages. When Brik responded that he was overworked, Bourdine told him in no uncertain terms to either shape up or face serious questions about his loyalty.

Shaken, Brik knew he had to break from the KGB. He turned to the only friend he felt he had in Canada—his lover in Kingston. At first, she laughed when he claimed to be an illegal Soviet spy. But Brik was able to convince her by describing his training and his work in minute detail. She made no promises, repeating that she could not leave her husband to be with him, but she urged Brik to go to the RCMP with his story. When he returned home to Montréal, Brik called the RCMP in Ottawa and confessed.

From the beginning, there was little doubt in Terry Guernsey's mind that he would run Brik as a double agent. Brik was given the codename "Gideon" and the operation was named "Keystone." Guernsey hoped to use Keystone to unmask other Soviet agents operating in Canada and to learn more about KGB spy craft in the process.

Several days after his confession, Brik, now known as Gideon, received orders to be at a pay phone on St. Catharine Street in Montréal. When the phone rang, Gideon answered and was told to go to a second pay phone a few blocks north on Sherbrooke. When he answered the second phone, he was told to walk to the Mount Royal Hotel. He had been given half of a Canadian one-dollar bill, and when he arrived at the hotel, a man approached and presented the other half.

"I was trying to tip the bellhop and he grabbed the bill and tore it right in two," said Charles Sweeney, an agent with the Security Service. He took Gideon up to a hotel room, interrogated him and introduced him to the process of being a double agent. Gideon could request an emergency meeting with Sweeney at any time, but would communicate mostly through the use of dead drops in and around Montréal.

Although the prospect of being a double agent and remaining in the West at first appealed to Gideon, it added another stressor to his already overwhelmed psyche. The new demands on his time made it almost impossible for him to visit his lover in Kingston. When he finally did manage to make the trip, Sweeney visited him shortly after his return to Montréal. The Security Service had tailed him to Kingston and recognized the woman as a potential hazard for their mission. If Gideon did eventually persuade the woman to run away with him, or if he confronted the husband directly, he risked exposure or possible harm. Guernsey arranged for the husband and wife to be transferred to a base in the Yukon Territory and out of Gideon's life forever.

Gideon was livid when he heard of the transfer. The end of the affair hit him hard, rattling nerves that were already frayed from the stress of leading a triple life. He called Sweeney for emergency meetings and threatened to quit, and then recanted when later confronted by Guernsey. On one occasion, Guernsey travelled to Montréal personally to read Gideon the riot act.

Ultimately, Gideon's emotional and highly volatile nature proved his undoing. One night while drowning his sorrows in gin at his Montréal flat, the spy picked up the phone and dialled the news desk of the *Montréal Gazette*.

"I have a story for you," he slurred into the mouthpiece. "I am a Russian spy."

The reporter at the other end of the line dismissed the caller as a drunken prankster and hung up the phone.

Someone else had been listening in. The RCMP had tapped Gideon's phones and bugged his apartment. The Mountie monitoring the conversation felt his heart skip a beat as he waited for the reporter's response. As soon as the call was over, the officer phoned headquarters in Ottawa. Within hours of the conversation, two agents appeared at Gideon's apartment, bundled him into a waiting car and drove him to Ottawa.

They kept him in a cell for several days, deprived of all human contact, his meals slipped to him through a slot in the door. He was led to believe that he had violated some Canadian law and was either going to be put on trial or sent back to Russia. After one particularly intense interrogation, Sweeney appeared. He told Gideon that he had just used the last of his political capital to convince the powers that be to drop the charges. In truth, there was never any potential for criminal charges. Guernsey and Sweeney merely wanted to scare Gideon into getting back on board with Operation Keystone.

Sweeney told the deeply relieved Gideon to wait while the Security Service tried to find him a ride home. The only man available for the job was a member of the Surveillance Unit, who had now been fully briefed on Keystone. His name was Jim Morrison.

Neither Gideon nor Morrison spoke much on the two-and-a-half -hour drive back to Montréal. Both were consumed by their own thoughts. Gideon sat in the passenger seat of the Buick, stewing silently over the events of the last few days. The possibility of being prosecuted for breaking Canadian law was daunting. His cover would be blown if he ended up in a Canadian jail, and when he got out—if he got out—the Soviets would be waiting for him.

Morrison also had personal demons to confront. The life he was leading, of high style and affluence, was essentially a lie. The Buck was his mother-in-law's, and the membership at the yacht club belonged to his father-in-law, a former admiral in the British navy. He had borrowed from as many creditors as he could, and was now reduced to borrowing money from friends. If word got back to his superiors about his financial situation, he could lose his job. Although he pondered the matter all the way to Montréal and all the way back, he could see no easy solution. His life was spinning away from him, and he had no idea how to stop it.

Once he returned to Ottawa, Morrison continued his work with the Security Service. When not out tailing his marks, he was still running Lemieux's errands. One of those errands involved a rather sensitive matter. The Security Service paid Bell Telephone $1000 per month to cover the costs of tapping the lines of suspected KGB agents. These payments were kept off the books, and it was Morrison's job to pick up the cash from Guernsey and deliver it to Bell's office.

The temptation proved too great for Morrison. He knew he'd never get away with stealing the cash, but he was a desperate man. So, one day in 1955, he took the cash from Guernsey and headed straight to his own bank. His creditors were temporarily satisfied, and a relieved Morrison was able to continue his lavish lifestyle for another month.

With one theft behind him, the second was even easier. Once again, his creditors quickly lapped up the money.

When Bell finally called to complain about the missing payments, Guernsey needed little of his crime-solving skill to figure out what had happened. After all, Morrison was the only one with access to the cash. That night, Guernsey went to Morrison's home and extracted a confession.

The matter was put before Cliff Harvison, now head of the Security Service. Harvison ordered Morrison to repay the full amount within one week or face criminal charges and expulsion from the RCMP.

The ultimatum sent Morrison into a panic. He had no way of scrounging up $2000 without selling his house or asking his in-laws for a loan. Then one day, as he cruised the streets of Ottawa, it dawned on him. There was a way he could raise the money, but he would have to be very careful about it.

❧◆❧

Gideon's five-day stint in jail jolted him back into action. When he returned to Montréal, he applied himself diligently to his work, both as a double agent and a photographer. Moscow responded to his growing progress by moving him one step up the espionage ladder. Gideon would now be in charge of actually "running" several agents in Canada.

The first agent, code-named "Green" by the RCMP and "Lind" by the KGB, was an employee for the A.V. Roe Aircraft Company in Toronto. The company was responsible for developing and producing the CF-105 Avro Arrow, widely considered the most advanced fighter jet of the Cold War. Lind delivered many of his reports from memory, although he was able to sneak out two sets of plans for the aircraft.

The KGB were so pleased with Gideon's work that they assigned four more agents to him. One was the owner of a TV and radio repair shop in Ottawa, two were women used by the KGB as couriers and one was a devoted communist living in Toronto. As 1954 rolled into 1955, the KGB also began to hint to Gideon that another illegal agent, codenamed "Hector," would soon join him. Gideon diligently passed the information along to the RCMP.

He was growing ever more confident now. When Nikolai Ostrovsky, the new KGB *rezident* in Ottawa told Gideon that he was being sent back to Moscow for advanced training and the chance to visit his wife, he suspected nothing. He asked the Security Service to plan an escape route for him should he be compromised, but he was certain he could outwit his KGB masters during his visit back home.

In August 1955, Gideon boarded a flight from Montréal to Brazil. After a brief layover, he connected to a flight to Helsinki, Finland, and from there flew to Moscow.

The Security Service never heard from him again.

At the time he had been caught pilfering cash, Morrison had been trailing the new Ottawa *rezident*, Nikolai Ostrovsky, for several weeks. The short, pot-bellied Russian spent most of his days reading magazines, going to movies in the afternoon, and drinking beer at the Grand Hotel.

On July 21, 1955, Morrison followed Ostrovsky into the Grand Hotel. He stood at the bar for a few minutes, nervously sipping a beer. Then he walked over to Ostrovsky's table and sat down.

"I believe I have some information that would be of interest to you," he told the Russian bluntly. Ostrovsky smiled warmly, his eyes registering only a mild flicker of surprise. He polished off his beer and then leaned in toward Morrison.

"Not here," he whispered. "Follow me."

Morrison followed the Russian to a spot below a bridge that spanned the Ottawa River. "I'm only doing this to help the Soviet cause," began the nervous police officer. But it didn't take long, Ostrovsky noticed, before he also mentioned that the information would cost $5000. The Russian told the Mountie he would see what he could do, and the two arranged to meet the following night in the countryside.

That night, on the deserted road near Aylmer, Ontario, Morrison unburdened himself to Ostrovsky. He told the Russian about Gideon and how the KGB illegal had been turned by the RCMP two years ago. Ostrovsky reacted calmly, absorbing the information before praising Morrison for his actions.

"A person in your position could do very well if he was willing to continue sharing information," Ostrovsky told him at the end of the meeting. He handed over a notebook and asked Morrison to jot down all the names of Security Service staff.

A few days later, Morrison turned up at Security Service headquarters with the $2000 he had been ordered to repay, and was allowed to continue in his capacity with the Security Service until Harvison had finished reviewing his file. During this time, Morrison met with Ostrovsky again and returned the notebook he had been given, which was filled with the names of Security Service personnel.

Eventually, Harvison decided that Morrison posed too much of a risk, given the recent thefts and his continuing financial difficulties. In the winter of 1955, he transferred Morrison out of the Security Service and assigned him to regular policing duties in Winnipeg.

Morrison's financial problems followed him to Manitoba. Within two years, he was back in trouble with his creditors. Needing money desperately, he sent a letter to an address in East Berlin requesting a meeting with Ostrovsky in Ottawa.

At the meeting, Ostrovsky quickly realized that Morrison had little to share. Ostrovsky hinted that the KGB would be eager to hear whether or not the Security Service was planning any sort of bugging operation against the new Soviet embassy. The old embassy had burned down the previous year, and the Soviets were building a new one. "That kind of information," said Ostrovsky, "I would gladly pay for."

Morrison gave it a try. He dropped in on an old friend from the Security Service, Leslie James Bennett, head of the Soviet desk in B division. While the two chatted, Morrison tried to pump Bennett for information. Although the Security Service was indeed planning a bugging operation with the help of MI5, Bennett was not one to talk out of school. He scrupulously evaded the subject, and Morrison left with nothing.

Nevertheless, Morrison demanded $5000 when he reported back to Ostrovsky. The Russian gave him $150 and told him the KGB would only pay for good information. If Morrison wanted real money, he would have to get himself transferred back to Ottawa or else find another source.

Of course, in the middle of Manitoba, Morrison had no access to any sensitive information. It didn't stop him from trying to extract more money from the Soviets, however.

But when he showed up for a third meeting in Ottawa, he was in for a surprise. Ostrovsky had been replaced by a handsome, young *rezident* named Rem Krassilnikov. Where Ostrovsky had been pleasant and warm, Krassilnikov was harsh and uncompromising. When Morrison demanded another $5000, Krassilnikov told him bluntly that the KGB would not pay him a dime without receiving anything in return. In that instant, Morrison knew he was finished. As he travelled back to his hotel room at the Chateau Laurier in Ottawa, an idea struck him. He could offer himself to the Security Service as a triple agent. He would tell his superiors about his meetings with Krassilnikov and offer his services as a conduit of false information. That way, he could still bilk the Russians out of money and regain his access to sensitive information. It was a ridiculous, hopeless scheme, but the police officer was blinded by his desperation.

Emboldened by his new plan, Morrison phoned Charles Sweeney from his hotel room shortly after 2:00 AM. As he rambled over the phone about the potential for deceiving the Russians, Morrison grew more and more confident that he had finally found a solution to his woes. The next morning two RCMP officers showed up at his hotel room and arrested him.

In the days of the Soviet Union, the KGB treated traitors ruthlessly. Interrogations were fierce; trials were swift; and the punishment was usually death. Gideon, however, was spared that fate. He had been arrested the moment he stepped off the plane in Moscow and had been brutally interrogated by the KGB. His saving grace was his cowardice; when the KGB offered him the chance to redeem himself and potentially save his own life, Gideon jumped at the chance.

He spent the next year helping the KGB identify foreign agents. Before he had left Canada, the Security Service had given a series of signals he could use if he needed to escape. Because Canada did not run agents in foreign countries, the British had agreed to help. Instead, Gideon decided to cooperate with the KGB. He was ordered to arrange a meeting with a British agent. KGB agents would wait at the assigned meeting place to photograph whoever showed up.

The KGB rewarded Gideon's efforts. At a secret session, the Military Collegium of the Supreme Court sentenced Gideon to 15 years in prison. He had escaped with his life.

Morrison found himself locked in a cell at RCMP headquarters in Ottawa. His former employers had now given him a code name—"Long Knife," and they began questioning him exhaustively about his activities.

For the first few days of his interrogation Long Knife stuck to his story, insisting that he was a triple agent. But on the ninth day, exhausted by the relentless questions and constant isolation, he began to talk.

He confessed to betraying Gideon to the KGB, as well as handing over the names of members of the Security Service. He admitted to receiving a total of $14,000 from the Russians in return for his information. He signed a full confession and was transferred to a jail in Winnipeg.

The Security Service was unsure of what to do with him. If they brought Long Knife to trial and exposed his treachery to the nation, it would be a public relations nightmare. Allowing him to escape without punishment, however, went against everything the RCMP stood for. In the end, Long Knife pleaded guilty to two counts of fraud for writing bad cheques. He was given a two-year suspended sentence, freed from jail and discharged from the RCMP.

Long Knife tried to fade away from his past by moving to British Columbia and working as a contractor, but history refused to let him go. In 1982, John Sawatsky published *For Services Rendered*, a biography of Leslie James Bennett. The book included a chapter on the Long Knife affair.

The nation howled when it learned that Long Knife had never been tried for his espionage crimes, and the government decided to act, albeit almost 30 years after the fact. In 1986, James Morrison, aka Long Knife, was charged with three counts under the Official Secrets Act. Although he first entered a plea of not guilty, several of his former colleagues identified him as the man in the interview on *The Fifth Estate*. Morrison promptly changed his plea to guilty.

On May 26, 1986, the disgraced Mountie, now 69 years old, was sentenced to 18 months in prison. After his release, no one knows what happened to him.

CHAPTER SIX

John Watkins
(1902–1964)

OCTOBER 1955

Quantities of vodka flowed that night, so the story goes.

The hours quickly blurred together with a haze of cigarette smoke and alcohol. To an outsider, the gathering looked like little more than a few rambunctious friends, laughing and talking, revelling in the promise of a night still young.

But this was no ordinary assembly. At the centre of room sat Nikita Khrushchev, Premier of the Soviet Union and arguably one of the two most powerful men on earth. Across from him sat Canada's Minister of External Affairs, Lester B. Pearson.

Pearson leaned forward as his host proposed yet another toast. Pearson had already noticed one of his aides stumble to the bathroom twice over the last hour, emerging each time wiping at his lips. Interpreters stood to either side of the table, filling in when the Russian or English became too colloquial for either side to understand.

Despite the informal appearance, the meeting was crucial. Lately, the Cold War had been anything but cold— it was nearing the boiling point. NATO and the

Eastern Bloc stared at each other from either side of the Iron Curtain, each waiting for the slightest slip that could justify war.

That war would bring casualties undreamed of, even by the standards of World War II. The U.S. had already flexed its nuclear muscles in 1945, at Hiroshima and Nagasaki. Four years later, the USSR successfully tested its first atomic bomb. The world faced the prospect of near-total annihilation in a seemingly inevitable war between communism and capitalism.

Pearson had come to Russia to try to ease the tensions. Khrushchev was hoping that Canada, sandwiched between the U.S. and USSR, would act as an intermediary in any future disputes.

Beside Pearson sat the man who had made the meeting possible. John Watkins had recently been promoted to the position of Canadian ambassador to Moscow. During his career at the embassy, he had developed an unrivalled level of friendship and access with communist party officials.

Khrushchev produced a fresh bottle and sloshed more vodka into everyone's glass. Pearson concentrated on picking up his drink without spilling, and then waited for the premier to speak.

"To the women we love," Khrushchev grumbled and then stopped, his smile widening, "even though not everyone in our company loves them was we do."

As he spoke, Khrushchev's eyes flicked briefly, almost imperceptibly, towards Watkins. The remark passed unnoticed in the drunken stupor that enveloped everyone in the room, although Pearson would later remark in his memoirs, "Watkins...looked less and less happy."

Had Pearson been paying attention that evening, John Watkins might have been "outed" long before the Russian bear could get its claws into him.

In the 1950s, two character flaws could instantly disqualify a person from public service in North America. The first, of course, was being a communist. The second was being gay.

Neither the government of the United States nor the more liberal government of Canada tolerated homosexuals working in their offices. A paper prepared by the RCMP in 1959, entitled "Security Cases Involving Character Weaknesses, with Special Reference to the Problem of Homosexuality," accused gay men and women of "instability, willing self-deceit, defiance toward society, a tendency to surround oneself with persons of similar propensities...none of which inspire the confidence one would expect to have in persons required to fill positions of trust and responsibility."

Between 1956 and 1963, the RCMP ferreted out and summarily sacked 100 alleged homosexuals from public service. In the official view of the day, homosexuality was morally reprehensible. Gay people were open to blackmail, making them a security risk. Tolerance and acceptance were distant concepts.

John Watkins was homosexual, but few people knew. The kindly, intelligent, diplomat had been born in 1902 on a farm in Ontario. He had a keen mind, a love of literature and art and a knack for languages.

He attended university on an academic scholarship, eventually earning a doctorate in Slavic languages at Cornell University. Once he had graduated, the physically unremarkable bachelor was recruited into the Department of External Affairs as a first secretary.

Watkins's worldly ways, as well as his gentlemanly conduct and proficiency with languages, contributed to his rapid rise in the ranks of Canada's diplomats. He was posted as charges d'affaires at Canada's embassy in Moscow in 1948, two years after joining the department.

Throughout the 1950s, Moscow was rated as a "hardship posting" by the department. The closed, hardened nature of Soviet society contributed to a sense of alienation at the embassy. KGB agents were omnipresent in Soviet life, seemingly standing on every corner, watching everyone.

Having distinguished himself in this uncompromising environment, Watkins was called back to Ottawa for service and then posted to Norway. Before long, the Canadian government promoted Watkins, at age 52, to the position of ambassador to the Soviet Union.

Although it was a time of great tension between East and West, the political realities of the conflict seemed lost on Watkins. He wrote flowery, detailed dispatches to Ottawa, documenting his day-to-day life in the USSR. He periodically scoffed at the security measures at the embassy, saying they were unsophisticated and a bit unsavoury. He dined with local intellectuals and artists throughout the city, listening as they voiced their supposed discontent with the Soviet system.

As his contacts grew in number, Watkins gradually gained unheard-of access to the highest corridors of power. Ministers and secretaries of the Politburo and Supreme Soviet returned his phone calls, held meetings with him and showed him documents that no other diplomat would ever have been allowed to see. Through it all, Watkins recognized no deceit on the part of the Russians. He believed that he was skilfully opening doors, rather than that they were being opened for him.

The Soviets knew that Watkins was a homosexual. The KGB had watched him since he was first posted to Moscow. Watkins met and befriended a man who worked at the Moscow Institute of History, Alexei Mihailovitch Gorbunov, whom he referred to in his dispatches as "Alyosha." The two frequently dined together in restaurants in Moscow, indulging in wine and good food as they argued about politics, history, art and literature. Watkins also relied on Alyosha as someone "who told me what's going on."

For an intellectual, Alyosha was well connected. He passed on information to Watkins about the workings of the Soviet government and arranged meetings with high-level bureaucrats. Later, Watkins confessed that Alyosha was also instrumental in arranging Lester Pearson's 1955 visit.

Another scholar at the Moscow Institute of History, Anatoly "Tolya" Nikitin, often joined Watkins and Alyosha. Whenever the three got together, Tolya and Alyosha dropped nuggets of information about the Soviet government, which Watkins later relayed to Ottawa.

If Watkins had been more prudent, he might have had misgivings about his two friends. As a rule, Soviet citizens were not permitted to casually associate with foreigners.

Neither Alyosha nor Tolya was who he claimed to be. Alyosha was, in fact, Oleg Gribanov of the Second Chief Directorate, the KGB agency responsible for intelligence operations against foreign diplomats. Tolya was also a senior KGB man, Anatoly Gorsky. The two agents were drawing Watkins deeper and deeper into their grasp, and they were getting ready to squeeze.

The KGB was notorious for seizing on people's weaknesses to turn them into agents. Their most common ploy was the "sex trap," in which they would confront a potential source with explicit evidence of his or her indiscretions. Help us, they'd say, and no one has to know what you've been up to.

Despite his intelligence and his diplomatic *savoir faire*, Watkins had not behaved himself in the Soviet Union. On a trip through Soviet Central Asia in January 1955, Watkins met a young man he could not ignore.

His name was Kamahl. He was employed on one of the Soviet Union's collective farms outside Dushanbe, Tajikistan, then known as Stalinabad. Watkins was unable to resist the muscular, sinewy frame and rugged good looks of the man 35 years his junior. They met at Watkins' hotel for dinner, then went up to his room and made love.

On the same trip, he shared a drunken, passionate tryst with a young poet in Tashkent, Uzbekistan. Although the KGB did not know of this encounter, they found out about Kamahl after other hotel guests reported the young man's presence in Watkins' room.

Consequently, when Kamahl called Watkins a few months later to say he would be visiting Moscow, the KGB was ready. Watkins jumped at the chance to see his lover again. The two spent a week together in Moscow, wandering the streets of the Soviet capital, seeing the sights. At night, when they retired to Kamahl's bedroom, the KGB was there, snapping photos.

The Soviets moved slowly. When the time came for Watkins to return to Ottawa and be replaced as ambassador, however, the KGB struck.

One late afternoon in 1956, Watkins travelled, at Gribonov's request, to the Russian's office at the Moscow Institute of History. The two chatted amiably for a few moments, exchanging pleasantries and personal updates. Eventually, the conversation died into an awkward silence, and Gribanov tapped a file on his desk.

"Something has come to my attention," he said, pushing the folder across the desk. "The KGB has been watching you."

As Watkins opened the file, his face fell. He flipped through photo after photo of Khamal entangled in his arms. He began to sweat profusely.

"Where did they get these?" he breathed in a panic.

"That, I do not know. I guess they have been tailing you for some time." Gribanov shook his head. "It is a despicable business, my friend. I cannot believe they would stoop to this. What happens in the privacy of a man's living quarters should not be fodder for spies," he spat out the last word like it was coated in venom.

"Who has seen this?" Watkins asked.

"At the moment, only a few agents, but I have taken the file out of their hands. They do not know I have it, nor should they," Gribanov leaned in towards Watkins. "You are a friend, and I wish to spare you the humiliation of exposure. If this became public…well, I think it would probably end your career."

"Alyosha, thank you, thank you," Watkins breathed. "You are a true friend."

"My friend, I need something from you in turn," Gribanov said. "I can keep this file easily out of sight, away from prying eyes who might seek to discredit you. But in exchange, I'll need your help."

"What do you mean?" Watkins asked.

"You are returning to Ottawa soon to take up a senior posting in your External Affairs department. Our new ambassador to Canada, Dimitri Chuvakin, is having a difficult time doing his work."

Gribanov sat upright and fixed Watkins with a penetrating glare.

"Be friendly to Chuvakin," he said. And with that, the meeting ended.

Watkins stared numbly through the windows of his car as he rode back to the embassy. Gribanov's intent was clear. The Soviets were not asking him to steal information, or smuggle microfilms of classified documents. They were looking for influence, for a way to promote the interests of the Soviet Union in a subtle, backhanded way. If Watkins didn't help them, his life as he knew it would be over.

He returned to Ottawa, unsure of what the future held in store for him.

In the early 1960s, KGB defectors began trickling through the Iron Curtain. Among the first was a KGB major named Anatoly Golitsin.

In December 1961, Golitsin presented himself to the CIA station in Helsinki, Finland. The Americans interrogated him for months. Among the many details they extracted was an allegation with dire implications for the government of Canada.

Golitsin told of a Canadian ambassador in Moscow, a homosexual who had been blackmailed by the KGB. Golitsin couldn't pin down the man's name, but he was sure the incident had occurred sometime during the 1950s.

The Americans finally let Canada in on their little secret, and in August 1962, they permitted an interview between Golitsin and Leslie James Bennett, head of the Soviet desk in B Division of the RCMP Security Service. In the meantime, the Security Service had launched Operation "Rock Bottom," its own effort to discover the identity of the ambassador in question.

The officers in charge of Rock Bottom faced an immense task. Because they had neither a specific name nor date to work with, they were forced to comb through hundreds of official embassy dispatches and records from the '50s. The paper chase produced few solid leads, but the focus of the investigation drifted toward one ambassador in particular—David Johnson, who had succeeded Watkins in 1956.

During Johnson's tenure at the embassy, a clerk had come to him with an embarrassing admission. KGB operatives had photographed the clerk in the company of a young man and were now trying to force him into their service. Rather than agree, he reported the incident to Johnson. The clerk believed that Johnson was also gay and hoped that he would simply hush up the matter to protect his own reputation. Instead, Johnson turned the clerk in to the RCMP.

The incident sparked a massive RCMP effort to uncover other homosexuals working in the public service. When they interrogated the clerk, he told them that Johnson had been suspected of being involved in an affair with another embassy official. The ambassador was recalled to Ottawa and interrogated by the RCMP. Although he offered his resignation, Johnson never admitted to being blackmailed by the KGB.

The KGB defectors kept coming. In the fall of 1963, Golitsin was followed by Yuri Krutkov, a Soviet writer who had turned himself into MI6 during a visit to London. The handsome Krutkov worked for the KGB in an unofficial capacity, entrapping Western female diplomatic staff in Moscow.

Krutkov was able to confirm Golitsin's story of a homosexual blackmail operation. Although, like Golitsin, he couldn't name the ambassador, he was able fix the time period more accurately, in the mid-to late 1950s.

The RCMP's outstanding questions were answered six months later when Yuri Nosenko, a KGB captain who had been passing information to the CIA for two years, unexpectedly defected to the West while in Geneva. He named Watkins specifically as the ambassador caught in the sex trap in Moscow. He also relayed the story of Khrushchev's provocative toast to Lester Pearson (now prime minister), in which he implied that not all of the men at the dinner liked women.

With Watkins positively identified, Bennett narrowed the RCMP's investigation. Try as they might, however, they could not produce any independent evidence that Watkins had acted inappropriately once he had returned to Ottawa. If anything, Watkins had gone to great lengths to avoid going anywhere near the Russians. During his posting in Ottawa, he had argued against several Soviet-friendly initiatives, including one that would have increased the complement of staffers allowed to work at the Soviet embassy (thus allowing the KGB to post more agents in Canada). Watkins had also spoken out against the proposed establishment of a Soviet consulate in Toronto.

One particular action, however, stood out for Bennett. Watkins had recommended increasing the distance Soviet-bloc embassy staff could travel unrestricted in and around Ottawa. In 1952, the Department of External Affairs had imposed a 120-kilometre restriction on all Soviet and Eastern European diplomatic staff. No one could travel outside that radius without the department's official permission.

Watkins' recommendation angered the RCMP. The loosened travel restrictions greatly aided Soviet intelligence operations throughout Canada, enabling agents to travel further afield to rendezvous points throughout the area.

But the Security Service was not so much worried about what Watkins did do as they were about what he could have done. He had access to classified information and policy documents, staff lists and directories, ciphers and codes as well as other information about the workings of the Department of External Affairs and the Canadian government. The Security Service could not prove whether or not Watkins had ever worked for the Soviets. In the world of policing and intelligence, absence of evidence did not mean the activity had not taken place. Once the shadow of suspicion was cast on someone, nothing could remove it.

One other glaring detail also stood out. It was now 1964, and Watkins had been serving as the ambassador to Denmark. He had suffered a heart attack and was slowly recovering during a succession of medical leaves in Paris. It had been eight years since the KGB had allegedly tried to entrap Watkins. If he had not reciprocated by working for the Soviets, why had the KGB not exposed his homosexuality?

In the end, the Security Service had little hard, concrete information on which to proceed. Late in the summer of 1964, Bennett decided it was time to travel to Paris and confront Watkins. Although the pale, sickly man at first admitted nothing, he eventually agreed to cooperate with the RCMP.

Watkins was whisked to a nearby CIA house. After several days of interrogation, the proceedings moved to London, and then in October to a Holiday Inn in Montréal.

Watkins was deeply embarrassed by his sexual orientation and his indiscretions in Moscow. Eventually, after Bennett worked hard to foster a bond, Watkins grudgingly confessed to being gay. Once the interrogation moved to Montréal, he also described the KGB's attempt at blackmail.

Throughout the entire questioning period Watkins steadfastly denied ever working for the Soviets in any capacity. The RCMP came at him with various allegations—some implied, some totally outrageous—in a vain attempt to rattle the 62-year-old man. Watkins denied the story of Khrushchev's little toast, denouncing it as a despicable attempt to discredit him. He admitted that he should have reported Gribanov's attempt at blackmail, but he was afraid of being branded a homosexual and a traitor. He defended himself competently against every accusation and ultimately revealed little.

On October 12, 1964, the interrogation was winding down. Bennett told Watkins that he could find no evidence that he had worked for the Soviets and that he was ready to file a report attesting to that fact. Although Watkins would never truly be free of the accusations against him, he would be allowed to live out the rest of his life in relative peace and solitude.

A relieved Watkins chatted amiably with his interrogators. He rambled on about his career, his experiences and the people he'd met. He talked almost as if his life were flashing before him.

Watkins paused briefly and reached for his cigarettes. Suddenly, he clutched his chest, his face contorted in unbelievable pain. He gasped, stumbled from his chair and collapsed on the floor of the hotel room, his last breath hissing through his teeth.

Bennett rushed to his side but could not find a pulse. Two police ambulance attendants responded quickly, but could not resuscitate him.

John Watkins was dead. So, too, were any chances of discovering what, if anything, he had done to betray his country.

In Canada, any person who dies in police custody is automatically entitled to both an autopsy and a coroner's inquest. John Watkins received neither.

For 15 years, the RCMP disseminated the story that Watkins had died during a farewell dinner with friends at a Montréal restaurant. They hid both the manner of his death and the fact that he was the subject of a police investigation. But such secrets do not stay buried long. In 1980, Canadian author Ian Adams gained legal access to Watkins' death certificate and instantly recognized the name of one of the witnesses who had signed the document, RCMP Corporal Harry Brandes.

When the revelation hit the press and the whole story came out, the Parti Québecois government of René Levesque immediately ordered a coroner's inquest. Senior Coroner Stanislas Dery found no evidence of foul play. The inquest, hindered by the RCMP's unwillingness to disclose the transcripts of Watkins' interrogation, found that Watkins had died of natural causes.

The story had other twists and turns. Author and historian David Sawatzky, in his 1982 book *For Services*

Rendered, described the 1972 interrogation and dismissal of Bennett, whom the RCMP had suspected of being a Soviet mole. During the interrogation, Bennett's questioners implied that, if Watkins had worked for the Soviets, Bennett would have wanted him eliminated before he could come clean about his activities. Perhaps, the RCMP suggested, Bennett had even switched Watkins' heart medication. Because no autopsy had been performed, the RCMP had no way to substantiate the claim.

Adams parlayed his discovery of Watkins' death certificate into both a novel and a television movie. His 1999 book, *Agent of Influence*, theorized that the CIA tried to exploit the Watkins situation in the hopes of bringing down the Pearson government. In 1964, the United States was unhappy with many of Canada's foreign policies, including its opposition to the war in Vietnam and its deal to sell Canadian wheat to the Soviet Union. Although Adams admits that many of the book's characters are either composite or fictional, he hopes that his book can "resurrect the spirit of a decent and honourable man who served his country well."

That Watkins was a victim of time and circumstance is indisputable. Whether or not Canada was a victim of John Watkins may never be fully proven.

CHAPTER SEVEN

Hugh Hambleton
(1922–??)

WHEN THE TWO PLAINCLOTHES NEW YORK POLICE DEPARTMENT (NYPD) officers trailing Rudi Herrmann saw him throw a length pipe out of his car window, they thought it was a bomb.

It was a cold, winter afternoon in North America's biggest city, and traffic was flowing surprisingly well for that time of day. Both detectives happened to be driving back to the station when they saw the car in front of them slow at a corner, next to a fire hydrant. Without stopping, the man driving the car in front of them rolled down a window and tossed something out.

The detectives didn't say a word to each other. The driver accelerated past Herrmann and forced him to the side of the road. Herrmann sat nervously in the car, trying to keep his cool, as a man in a suit and tie walked up along side his car. The second walked towards the fire hydrant.

"Sir," the detective said as he approached. "Seems you lost something out your window there."

"Just garbage," Herrmann responded quickly. "I can go back and pick it up, if you want."

"Hey!" The second detective shouted. "Don't let him go anywhere!"

He lifted the pipe gingerly from the concrete. It wasn't a bomb; neither end was capped. He rotated the cylinder so he could look into it, and saw something wrapped inside. Reaching in with his fingers, he pulled out a piece of paper.

"Whattaya got?" the detective standing beside Herrmann asked. Rudi's heart raced as he watched the other detective in his rear-view mirror.

"Looks like some sort of message," the other policeman responded, unrolling the document.

It contained only numbers and letters, joined together in an almost random fashion. Though he was no intelligence agent, the detective recognized a coded message when he saw one. He showed the paper to his partner. They conferred quietly for a moment and then took Herrmann back to their headquarters.

The Federal Bureau of Investigation (FBI) arrived later that afternoon, bundling Herrmann quietly off to another building. For two days, they bombarded him with questions about his background. By the end of the second day, Rudi was exhausted. It was obvious the Americans weren't going to let him go.

Starting at the beginning, Herrmann began to tell his story to his captors. He was an agent in the KGB, an "illegal," in charge of several Soviet spy networks in North America. He revealed his legend, his codes and his contacts throughout the U.S. He described not only the agents he ran in the States, but in Canada as well.

Herrmann swallowed, and then began telling the FBI about Hugh Hambleton.

For as long as Hugh Hambleton could remember, he'd been surrounded by people. Born in Ottawa in 1922, the Canadian lad had spent most of his youth travelling the world. His father George, a press correspondent, was posted to France for most of the 1920s and some of the 1930s. When young "Hugo" was not attending primary school in France, his parents shipped him to California where he learned Spanish. Almost from the moment he was born, his mother Bessie had wanted nothing but the best for her son. Education, she believed, was a key component of that dream.

The family settled in a large house on Ruskin Avenue in Ottawa, and their home soon became a gathering place for some of the Canadian capital's political and diplomatic elite. Seldom did a weekend go by, it seemed, when Hugo and his sister Josephine were not rubbing elbows with ambassadors, politicians and high-level bureaucrats. In the Hambleton household, knowledge and experience flowed, and politics and history were discussed freely. There, Hugo felt both valued and special. As he would later tell one of his boyhood friends, Leo Heaps, "To be important, to have people pay attention to you, that's what counts in life."

But by the 1940s, Hugo, like many young Canadian men, was looking to serve overseas. Adolf Hitler's military forces were engulfing Europe, butchering and killing as they went. Poland, Belgium and Holland had all fallen swiftly under the Nazi juggernaut, and

France's ancient defences were crumbling. As the Wehrmacht marched into Paris, French patriots disappeared underground. Intent on fighting the Germans from the inside, they formed the Free French under the direction of Charles De Gaulle.

Although Hugo had originally been rejected for a position in the Free French Ambulance Corps, his parents, using their political connections, managed to find their son a place with the underground army's colonial headquarters in Algiers. At first his duties were mostly administrative, but he soon rose through the ranks. He became a liaison officer with the 103rd U.S. Army Division in 1944, part of the Allied thrust that was sweeping the Germans back to their pre-war borders. By war's end, Hugo had stepped up even further. He was interrogating prisoners of war, as well as analyzing intelligence reports, for the Canadian army.

When he returned to Ottawa, he found his family home much as he'd left it. There were still parties, important events and heated discussions. The world, however, was changing, and in Bessie Hambleton's opinion, it was changing for the better. As the USSR used its post-war foothold to spread its Communist ideals throughout Eastern Europe, the Cold War began to rage. Igor Gouzenko, a young GRU intelligence clerk with the Soviet Embassy in Ottawa, defected with papers exposing a Soviet spy ring in Canada and several other Western countries. The Europe that had been unified by force under Hitler was now divided by ideology, as capitalism and communism faced off.

Upon returning from Europe, Hugo completed his Bachelor of Arts at Ottawa University and found work

with the National Film Board. In 1948, he married
Thérèse Beaudoin, the daughter of a high-level public
servant in the Ministry of Defence.

The day-to-day life of a married staffer was not,
however, what Hugo was looking for in life. The crav-
ing for significance, to be someone who accomplished
much in life, pulled at him constantly. He became fas-
cinated by his studies in history and economics, and
the prospect of a scholarly life appealed to him. But
little glory could be had in essays and academic books.
Excitement and purpose, it seemed, were two paths in
his life that would never cross.

In 1949, Hugo met someone who changed the
course of his entire life. It was April, and his mother
was hosting yet another soiree with Ottawa's crème
de la crème. When he arrived at home, his mother
promptly introduced him to Vladimir Borodin, the
cultural attaché from the Soviet embassy.

Bessie had met Borodin at a function at the Chilean
embassy the week before and had invited him to her
party. Based on her initial impressions, Bessie had a
feeling the skinny Russian and her son would get
along well. The two spent much of the evening chatting and agreed to meet for lunch the following day.
That weekend, Borodin joined the Hambleton family
for a day trip to their cottage at Meech Lake.

As Bessie and the rest of the family busied themselves in the cottage, Borodin and Hugo went for a
walk. As they strolled idly through open fields, Borodin
began to speak about the differences between Canada
and the Soviet Union. Hugo listened intently, as the
Russian turned and looked at him.

"It would be, I think, in both our countries' best interests if there were people willing to bridge that gap," he said. "I hope that, at some point, you might be one of those people."

The sentiment was more than mere ideological small talk; Borodin was no cultural attaché. He was, in fact, the chief *rezident* of the KGB's First Chief Directorate, the man responsible for recruiting and running spy networks in Canada. He saw in Hugo a quiet man with ambition who could be easily persuaded to work for the KGB.

Although he would later claim he shared no ideological conviction with Borodin or the Soviets, evidence later suggested otherwise. In a book released in 1999 called *The Mitrokhin Archive*, Vasili Mitrokhin, a former KGB agent who later defected to the West, revealed that Hambleton returned from the war a devoted communist. He attended meetings of the Canadian Communist Party, and before Borodin approached him at his mother's party, he was "talent scouted" by members of the organization.

Hugo agreed, and the two left it at that. Over the next two years, Borodin and Hugo met three more times. Each time, Borodin probed the Canadian's political beliefs and appealed to his vanity. Hugo responded to Borodin's flattery. He went so far as to steal a document detailing the test results of a new sonar unit for the Canadian Navy and gave it to the Russian.

"It would be helpful," Borodin suggested on one occasion, "if you pursued a career in government or even politics. We could work even more closely together."

Hugo was receptive to the idea, but he had other things to accomplish first. He had completed a Master's degree at the University of the Americas in Mexico and wanted very much to further his education in Europe. In 1952, he moved to Paris with Thérèse to continue his studies at the Sorbonne.

For three years, Hugo buried himself in the work of a scholar. Then, in 1955, with no forewarning, Borodin showed up on his doorstep. He had a friend in tow, whom he referred to only as "Paul." The three men visited briefly, then agreed to meet for lunch the following week.

At the café, the two Russians began to press Hugo more aggressively. They flattered him as a scholar and student and again expressed their wish for mutual cooperation between the West and the Soviet Union. At the end of the meal, Paul urged Hugo to apply for a job at the Paris headquarters of the North Atlantic Treaty Organization (NATO).

Hugo agreed. He felt a bond between himself and Paul, as well as with Borodin, and was eager to please both. He applied for a position as an economic analyst in April 1955 and, in November 1956, received his NATO security clearance.

The Soviets started him off slowly, so as not to arouse suspicion. The KGB opened a file on Hambleton, giving him the codename "Rimen" (which was later changed to "Radov"). They arranged to meet every other Thursday at 8:00 PM at a series of metro stations in Paris. The rendezvous would take place at one station on one Thursday, then at the next station down the line the following Thursday and so on. If, for any reason, either man missed a meeting

they would meet two weeks later at the next scheduled stop.

NATO documents were classified according to four
levels of secrecy: restricted, confidential, secret and,
finally, cosmic, the most secret of all documents. Paul
first asked Hugo to read restricted documents, mem-
orize them and then summarize them at their next
meeting. The information for the first few weeks
included coal production levels, as well as analysis of
political groups in NATO countries.

Hugo responded tentatively at first. For his first few
days at NATO, he considered simply telling his boss
what was going on. But after the first meeting with
Paul, he became addicted to the spy life. His skin tingled with excitement as he rode the metro every other
Thursday, trying to look as inconspicuous as possible.
Paul would always take him to an upscale restaurant
to pick his brain and praise him for his work.

Hugo's excitement ballooned one evening when
Paul passed him a 35mm camera and several rolls of
film. The Soviets now wanted him to smuggle documents out of the office, photograph them and then
hand over the film. Hugo responded with great
enthusiasm, photographing 70 documents in the
first month.

Over time, Hugo was able to pass along ever more
important information. He had been at NATO long
enough to sign out cosmic documents with analyses
of NATO's military capability. On at least one occasion,
Hugo was able to smuggle out and photograph a list of
NATO intelligence agents operating in both Estonia
and Lithuania.

The work seemed mundane, but it was actually quite risky. Guards at NATO headquarters had the authority to search briefcases at any time. Despite a few close calls, however, Hugo was never searched.

Hugo's life had changed as a result of the endless hours spent in his study, peering over the lens of camera. Thérèse had left, taking their son with her. In 1959 Hugo married again, a young lady named Fiorella Marcia, whom he had met during his travels.

That same year, Hugo's experience with the Soviets intensified. On a picnic lunch with Paul and a third man, Hugo was handed a briefcase containing a radio, as well as several one-time cipher pads and codebooks. The third man showed Hugo how to work the short-wave radio, not that he really needed instruction. He had been using short-wave radios since his childhood, listening eagerly to news broadcasts from around the world.

This device, however, was more complex. Instead of receiving the usual Morse code broadcasts, this radio would receive what sounded like a series of random sounds. Hugo would record the broadcasts onto audiocassettes that would be transformed into Morse code when exposed to a magnet. Although he had previously chosen what documents he would smuggle out of NATO headquarters, the Soviets now asked him for specific documents. It would later be revealed that one of NATO's chief archivists was actually a KGB agent.

Although Fiorella bore him a son in 1960, Hambleton's zeal for espionage did not diminish. Nor was he intimidated by the fact that spies could still be executed in many NATO countries, including France. He never believed he was doing anything to hurt his native country of Canada; he was simply helping forge a sense of trust and mutual cooperation between two warring parties.

His clandestine activities made him feel special, even if he couldn't share that feeling with anyone. Every radio transmission, every dead drop of film, every smuggled document sent a shiver of pure joy up his spine. The adrenaline coursing through his system was a drug, and Hugo was hooked on it.

Some of Hambleton's encounters could have come straight out of the movies. In Vienna, in 1960, he approached a fellow agent and asked him, "Do you have any etchings in Paris for me?" The man completed the code phrase with, "No, I have no etchings in Paris. But I do have some in London."

After five years, however, Hugo's love of adrenaline was no longer enough to keep him from pursuing his scholarly ambition. He had had all he could take of NATO. A scandal had swept over the headquarters. His boss, John Licence, had been caught in a homosexual affair, regarded at the time as a serious offence and a threat to security. Hugo used the affair to his own advantage, telling Paul that he feared capture because of the increased security measures. He also told Paul that he had always intended to complete a second Ph.D. at the prestigious London School of Economics (LSE), and he figured now was the time to do it. Surprisingly, Paul agreed with him and wished him luck.

Upon returning home from his meeting, Hambleton short-circuited his short-wave radio and destroyed it, along with his camera, cipher pads and codebooks, in a thickly forested area outside Paris. He and Fiorella moved to London shortly afterward, so that Hugo could begin his studies in earnest.

In London, Hugo quickly forgot about the excitement of the spy world and threw himself into his post-doctoral work. He became increasingly distant from Fiorella, in much the same way that he had gradually lost interest in Thérèse. As he lay in bed at night, he would think longingly back to his life as a spy. Maybe someday he would experience that thrill again, he thought, but not now.

The KGB, however, had not forgotten him. Borodin showed up in London in 1962 for a brief, unexpected visit at Hambleton's home, and the two spent an afternoon catching up. Several months later, while Hugo vacationed at his family's property in Torremolinos, Spain, he and Paul arranged to have dinner together. They enjoyed a fine meal and, at Paul's urging, went to a local strip club. Hugo thought the two were just catching up on old times, not knowing that Paul carried a poison-tipped pen in his jacket. Paul had been sent to assess whether or not Hambleton posed an intelligence risk to the KGB. If so, he was ordered to kill him with the pen. Luckily for Hugo, Paul concluded Hugo posed no such risk.

By 1964, Hugo completed his post-doctorate at LSE and was hired as an economics professor at Laval University in Québec City. Although the KGB tried to keep him involved in their world, Hugo was no longer interested. During his first three years back in Canada, he met with his controller only three times. The KGB had asked him to keep an eye out for potential student and faculty subversives at the university, but Hugo soon lost interest. After the third meeting, in 1965, Hugo stopped attending altogether. It was then the

KGB decided to activate one of its most valuable assets in North America to remind Hugo of his commitments.

Rudi Hermann worked at Harold's Famous Delicatessen, but he was far from a typical restaurateur. He wasn't even German, as he claimed. His name had been plucked from the pocket of a dead Sudeten German in World War II. Rudi Hermann was, in fact, Ludek Zemenek, a Czech national who had been recruited into the KGB from the Czech border guards.

Herrmann had been trained by the Soviets as an "Illegal," an agent covered by a false identity, sent overseas for intelligence purposes. His main mission was to blend in, to establish himself as a good Canadian citizen who paid his taxes on time and cheered for the Maple Leafs. When the time was right, the KGB would give him his orders.

Those orders came in 1967, shortly after Herrmann had sold the deli on Moscow's orders and moved to New York City, along with his wife Inga, (also an illegal) and their son Peter. Herrmann crossed the U.S.-Canadian border in April 1967 and visited Hugo at his Laval office. Under cover, Hermann claimed to be working on a film about former Québec Premier Maurice Duplessis.

When the two met later that night for dinner at Quebec's resplendent Chateau Frontenac, Herrmann leaned toward Hugo and whispered, "We have a mutual friend. His name is Paul." The name hit Hugo like an electric shock. He knew instantly that the KGB wanted him back, and he did not hesitate to agree.

For the first two years of his renewed career in espionage, Hambleton prepared reports on Canadian political and military developments, leaving them at dead drops along the highway between Montréal and Ottawa. He and Rudi saw each other frequently, meeting at the Chateau Frontenac for lavish dinners. In 1970, however, Hugo was instructed to travel again to Vienna, where he met his old friend Paul.

Hugo had always liked and respected Paul and was happy to see him again. Paul asked Hugo to take on a new and more elaborate assignment. The Soviets were looking for a way to insert agents amongst the approximately 300,000 Russian Jews emmigrating to Israel. Would Hugo go to Israel and prepare a report on how to best accomplish this? As always, Hugo could not say no to Paul.

The ruse was quite simple. Hugo had been planning to do some research in Turkey, and it would be easy enough to take a quick side trip to Israel. Later, Paul later told him that his report had been received with great zeal in Moscow and had even been read by several members of the Politburo, the supreme Soviet governing body.

Hugo's trip to Israel had been a triumph, but it also marked the beginning of the end of his anonymity as a spy. Shortly after the visit, the Mossad, Israel's spy agency, conducted its own investigation into Hugo's background. Although the investigation began in 1970, the Mossad never shared its suspicions with the RCMP.

Back in Canada, Hugo's life was about to take on an even more international flavour. In 1971, the Canadian International Development Agency (CIDA) appointed him as an economic advisor to Peru's leader, General Velasco Alvarado. His KGB controllers were thrilled when Hambleton became part of the general's inner circle. During his time in Peru, the country's economic ties gradually shifted away from the West and toward the Soviet Union.

When Alvarado grew ill and his regime was replaced by a civilian government, Hugo returned to Canada. In 1973, CIDA again asked Hugo to travel abroad, this time to help institute agricultural reform in the impoverished Caribbean nation of Haiti. By this time, he and Fiorella had divorced, leaving him with few familial ties in Canada.

While in Haiti, Hugo prepared another report for the KGB. Rudi occasionally visited him in Port-au-Prince, Haiti's capital.

When Hugo's tenure in Haiti finished in 1975, he travelled again to Israel to visit friends. During this visit, the Mossad kept him under constant surveillance.

The Israelis were not the only ones watching Hambleton. While travelling by train to Vienna from Israel to meet Paul, Hugo met a vibrant young woman named Lili. Because he had a few days to spare, he decided to stop over in Belgrade, Yugoslavia, to spend more time with her. One night, however, he was picked up by the KOS, the Yugoslavian counter-intelligence. They interrogated him and then ordered him to leave the country.

Neither Paul nor Hugo, however, paid much attention to the incident. Instead, within hours of meeting Paul in Vienna, Hugo was taken by limousine to an airport in Prague and bundled aboard a military flight to Moscow. He spent the next week with KGB, political and military officials, learning more about invisible inks, codes and technology. He later claimed he dined with Yuri Andropov, the head of the KGB, who later became General Secretary of the Politburo.

KGB agents also schooled him the use of a *luminaire*, a device that decrypted music from short-wave broadcasts into alphanumeric groupings that could then be decoded. These devices, Hugo was told, were reserved for only the most important agents. After he returned to Montréal, Hugo was given his very own *luminaire* in a rendezvous in an underground parking garage.

Although he continued to send reports to the Soviets, including one on South Africa's nuclear capability, Hugo quickly disappeared back into the academic world at Laval. He maintained a correspondence with Lili, who visited him in 1976.

He took a sabbatical year in 1978, purportedly to analyze oil production in the Middle East. This dovetailed well with his espionage duties—preparing reports on the Egyptian economy and on Israel's vulnerability to an oil embargo.

Hugo's cover, however, had long since been blown. In 1977, the police had caught Rudi Herrmann trying to leave a secret message at a dead-drop site in New York. During two days of interrogation, he was promised immunity and a new life in America for him and his family if he cooperated. Herrmann began to name names and among the first was Hugh Hambleton. In May 1978, the CIA allowed two RCMP Security Service officers to videotape an interview with Herrmann at a farmhouse in Maryland.

The FBI tried to turn Herrmann and run him as a double agent, but the Czech was able to insert small signals into his communications with Moscow to inform the KGB that he had been caught. In October

1978, Hugo was summoned to Vienna for an urgent meeting with Paul. Paul got right to the point.

"You may be in danger," he said perfunctorily. "Defect now. You will be safe in Moscow. I am leaving for Bratislava immediately. You can come with me if you wish."

Hugo, however, declined Paul's offer, unwilling to walk away from his job, his mother and his son. He gave his friend a farewell embrace and walked back to his hotel. They never saw one another again.

Hugo was wrong, however, if he thought the RCMP would ignore him. The force had spent the bulk of the summer investigating him. They placed him under surveillance when he returned from sabbatical in 1979 and, after a month, they were ready to act. On November 4, just after 7:00 AM, Hugo answered a knock at his apartment door in Québec City. It was the police, armed with a search warrant.

The RCMP detained Hambleton for questioning and showed photos of him visiting his drop sites between Montréal and Ottawa shortly after he had arrived. Hambleton knew he had been found out, but he was careful in his confession. He admitted to spying while in Canada, but judiciously failed to mention anything about his years at NATO. He sprinkled his confession with fiction about whom he had spoken with, who his controllers were and what he had actually done.

After 13 interrogations that stretched into 1980, the Solicitor General of Canada made a decision that left the Mounties swearing under their breath. He offered Hambleton immunity in exchange for his testimony, in the hope that he would expose other spies in Canada.

The case against Hambleton was relatively weak. Although he had transmitted information to a foreign power, according to the Official Secrets Act he could only be found guilty of espionage if that information had been secret. Much of the information Hugo had passed along after his NATO years was freely available to the public.

Hambleton was also incapable of betraying other spies, because Herrmann had essentially been his only contact in North America. After Hambleton signed the document guaranteeing his immunity, he became more cooperative. He confessed his activities during his time with NATO and corrected several mistruths he had told in earlier interrogations.

Canada's decision not to prosecute Hambleton shocked the Americans and the British. The U.S. decided to act. In 1980, they produced Rudi Herrmann for a press conference in which he named Hambleton as one of his agents. The result was sensational. Stories about Hambleton made the front pages of papers across the country. In interviews, Hugo said he was not surprised that he was not being prosecuted. "A spy is someone who regularly gets secret material, passes it on, takes orders and gets paid for it," he said. "I have never been paid." That, however, was a lie. In the late 1970s, the KGB had paid Hambleton at least $18,000 for his work.

At first, Hugo revelled in the attention. At long last he had achieved his life's goal of being important and recognized by people. Attendance at his lectures exploded, and he quickly became one of the most popular professors on campus. The RCMP, as well as other foreign agencies, continued to interrogate him.

At first, he found the attention flattering, but by 1981 it became a burden.

In June 1982, Hambleton and his youngest son boarded a flight to London, despite RCMP warnings that his immunity did not extend beyond Canada's borders. Hugo hoped to cash in on Paul's offer of sanctuary in Moscow, where he could live in relative obscurity.

The moment Hugo stepped off the plane at Heathrow, however, he was paged over the intercom. When he reported to the airport lounge, two detectives informed him he was not welcome in Britain. He could turn around and catch the next flight to Canada or be arrested. Incredibly, Hambleton gave one of the detectives the address of his hotel and said that he would stay in London.

Hugo spent his first day in London waiting to be contacted, but the KGB had no further interest in him. Because he had already been captured and unburdened himself of all of his secrets, they had no reason to bring him in from the cold. The next morning, British authorities arrested him, and on June 27, he was officially charged with two violations of the Official Secrets Act.

The trial, which began on November 29, was a short affair. With access to the files of both the RCMP and Britain's two security services, Attorney General Michael Hoover easily tore Hambleton's story to shreds on the witness stand. Four days into the trial, Hugo made the incredible pronouncement that he had actually been working as a double agent for the Canadians and the French against the KGB. He named Jean Mason and Jacques Laliberté as his respective controllers in Canada and France but could not prove the existence of either. Canadian and French officials resoundingly denied his claims. Exhausted, his story in tatters, Hambleton changed his plea. He declared himself guilty of one of the charges against him, and the second was dismissed.

Hugh Hambleton, the 60-year-old economics professor who only wanted to be noticed, to be seen, to be recognized and remembered, was sentenced to 10 years in prison.

In 1986, he was transferred to a Canadian prison on humanitarian grounds, to be closer to his ailing mother. He spent his days and nights listening to a shortwave radio in his cell. The static and voices from around the world brought back memories of more exciting times, but Hambleton never told anyone whether or not sacrificing his loyalty to his country had been worth the notoriety he received.

In 1989, after serving two-thirds of his sentence, Hambleton was released from prison and settled outside Ottawa. He disappeared into a life of obscurity. It is not known at the time of this writing whether or not he is still alive.

CHAPTER EIGHT

Joint Task Force Two

October 24, 2001

A movie played on board the polaris airbus parked on the tarmac at the Ottawa Macdonald-Cartier International Airport.

Approximately 80 passengers sat in their seats, their attention shifting between the movie that played on a wall-mounted screen and the eight armed men patrolling the aisles. The gunfire on the screen echoed the threats the gunmen made as they walked down the aisle.

"If anybody f***ing moves, they die!" shouted one of the men, gripping a pipe bomb in one of his hands. "Try anything and I'll blow this whole f***ing plane apart."

The men had hijacked the plane earlier that evening shortly after the passengers had boarded. Negotiators, who tried to establish communications with the hijackers, were rebuffed or ignored. One movie had played all the way through and a second, *Mission: Impossible II*, had started. The hostages sat perfectly still in their seats as instructed, concentrating on the movie, trying not to think about what might happen to them.

As the hours crept by, a few of the gunmen were slowly coming unglued. The man with the pipe bomb walked the aisles more and more feverishly, waving the incendiary device in the air, shouting warnings and threats. Suddenly, he stood at the front of the plane and held up the bomb for all to see.

"We're all going to f***ing burn!" he screamed.

At that moment, the lights went out. The airplane generators died with a fading moan, and the movie screen went black. The airplane was momentarily silent. Each hostage felt his and her skin tingle in the inky darkness.

"Nobody..." the man with the bomb started but was cut off by a loud bang. Sharp beams of white light cut through the darkness, blinding everyone on board.

"Keep your heads down!" a man shouted from the front of the aircraft. He punctuated his order with a staccato burst from his submachine gun. The hijacker with the pipe bomb was the first to go down.

From nowhere, a team of furtive figures in black appeared in the aircraft. The hijackers yelled, some raising their guns, but they quickly fell to the ground under a hail of bullets. A few hostages looked up but could see little except for six men, dressed in black from head to toe, sweeping the cabin with battle lights slung under the barrels of their guns.

Abruptly, the gunfire died.

"Clear!" a voice shouted, and other voices echoed the word. The battle lights clicked off, and the interior of the plane was plunged once again into darkness. The hostages began to move a little. Some stood, trying to see what was going on.

The airplane lights snapped back on. The hostages all grinned at one another despite their trembling hands and flushed faces.

The hijacker with the pipe bomb struggled to his feet, groaning as he did so. He wiped at the purple smear of paint that now decorated his chest, right over his heart. The other hijackers also rose, one by one, sporting similar stains on their jackets.

The 80 Canadian Forces (CF) reservists who had volunteered to play hostages peered through the aircraft windows, looking for a sign of their saviours. All they saw was a collection of vehicles sitting on the tarmac outside.

As quickly as they had appeared, the men of Joint Task Force Two—"The Men in Black"—had faded away.

In hindsight, the media should have known before they were told.

On January 22, 2002, newspapers around the world ran a photo from the front lines of the war in Afghanistan. The picture, snapped by an Associated Press photographer, depicted two soldiers in forest green fatigues, balaclavas covering their faces, propelling two men of Afghani descent from the back of a helicopter that had landed at a base in Kandahar. The photo's caption credited U.S. Special Forces with capturing two members of the Taliban.

Days later, it was revealed that the soldiers depicted in the photo were, in fact, members of Canada's ultrasecret special forces unit, Joint Task Force Two (JTF2).

Three months earlier, the government had made an uncharacteristic move, publicly announcing that JTF2 was being deployed to Afghanistan. The unit was sent as part of Canada's contributions to the international effort to unseat the Taliban and hunt down members of Al-Qaeda, the terrorist organization that had claimed responsibility for the attacks of September 11, 2001.

Reporters across the country kicked themselves over the photograph, for one obvious reason—the uniforms. Much had been made in the press of the fact that Canadian troops deployed Afghanistan had not been issued desert camouflage. All they had were their standard forest green uniforms, which, critics feared, would make them easy targets in Afghanistan's decidedly un-green environment.

Outside Parliament, Defence Minister Art Eggleton confirmed that the photographed soldiers were indeed members of JTF2.

"Did you notice the fact they had forest green uniforms?" Eggleton asked the press during a scrum outside the House of Commons. "Well, they were Canadian. JTF2."

The startling admission was the first time the Canadian government had ever acknowledged the activities of the unit, which was now cutting its teeth in the first operational deployment of its eight-year history.

In the 1980s, the Canadian government realized it lacked an effective force to battle acts of terrorism on its own soil. That fact was driven home in 1985 when three armed terrorists affiliated with the Armenian Revolutionary Army attacked the Turkish embassy in Ottawa, killing one security guard. The men later surrendered to members of the Ontario Provincial Police (OPP), but if the crisis had been drawn out, the only other option would have been to call in local OPP and RCMP SWAT units. SWAT officers are trained to deal with high-risk raids and takedowns, but they lack the elite training of counter-terrorism units in other countries, such as the SAS (Britain), Delta Force and SEAL Team Six (U.S.) and GSG-9 (Germany).

The government acted quickly. It commissioned a specialized force in the RCMP, known as the Special Emergency Response Team (SERT), to assume the counter-terrorism role. The decision, however, quickly came under fire from both the police and the CF. All of SERT's international counterparts were military units, not police units. It seemed counter-intuitive, some argued, to give peace officers the task of killing on sight. Although the unit was deployed to Calgary as security for the 1988 Olympic Winter Games, SERT's fate was sealed the moment the first voice of dissent spoke up. Despite several media events in which SERT officers rappelled from heli-copters, raided buses and aircraft and moved with swift, lethal speed through their training facility at Dwyer Hill in Ontario, the government immediately began to contemplate shifting the counter-terrorism responsibility to the military. In 1992, Deputy Minis-ter of Defence Robert Fowler announced SERT would be disbanded and a military unit formed in its place.

Establishing a specialized military unit appealed to the government on several levels. First, it obviated the need to train police officers to "shoot to kill," shifting that specialty to soldiers who were already trained to do so. Secondly, the CF could provide a steadier stream of well-trained recruits than the RCMP. The unit also had the potential to establish itself as a spe-cial forces unit similar to the SAS or U.S. Special Forces, trained not only in hostage rescue, but in "green ops," or special missions behind enemy lines. Military planners in the CF decided that the unit, christened JTF2, would operate in a similar fashion to the SAS, in small two- or four-man units known as "bricks." Each JTF2 soldier was to be a veteran of the CF and display maturity and the ability to think under pressure, as well as have solid shooting skills and quick reflexes.

The first 1000 recruits, most of whom came from either the Canadian Airborne Regiment or the Princess Patricia's Canadian Light Infantry, underwent a strenuous screening process. After interviews and security checks, each volunteer was put through a gruelling five-day physical evaluation. Most were RTUed (Returned to Unit). Those few deemed fit to advance began training in assault tactics, weapons and sniper work. By the end of the advanced training, barely one in ten of the original recruits made it into JTF2. In the spring of 1993, the CF officially activated the elite commando unit.

The ongoing training of JTF2 soldiers was as rigorous as the qualifying process. Soldiers were on call 24 hours a day, seven days a week, often paged to the base in the middle of the night to respond to mock crises. The former SERT training facility at Dwyer Hill was upgraded to accommodate the JTF2 commandos. Soldiers spent their days in a million-dollar shooting range, honing their skills with MP-5 submachine guns and Sig Sauer side arms. They acquired a DC-9 aircraft and an old Greyhound bus to practice hostage takedowns. They rehearsed assaults at a four-storey building at the complex and ran drills in a "killing house," a cavernous warehouse in which any combat environment could be simulated.

Soldiers were trained in unarmed combat, knife fighting, mountain climbing and arctic survival, as well as "fast-roping" from the unit's three Twin Huey helicopters.

The unit's strength lay in using surprise and speed to overwhelm the enemy. If called upon to assault a building or a hijacked vehicle, JTF2 soldiers followed a series of distinct steps. First, the unit gathered as much intelligence as possible about the hijackers' whereabouts and identified the best points of entry. The soldiers then blew open the doors or walls with breach charges and tossed in "flash-bang" grenades, which emit a bright light and thunderous clap to momentarily disorient the enemy. The second the grenades went off, the soldiers poured in through their points of entry. They searched each room in seconds, quickly distinguishing hostage-takers from hostages, and eliminated each enemy with a "double-tap," a two-round volley through the heart or head.

Although the exercises and practice kept them sharp, Canada's commandos itched to put their skills to the test in the real world, to prove themselves in an actual military situation. That time came on Canadian soil in 1994, when the government began planning a joint military-police operation against the Mohawk warriors involved in the Oka crisis in 1990. Although the warriors had been allowed to return to their reserves peacefully, some were still smuggling cigarettes and weapons across the U.S.-Canadian border. Determined to quash such criminal activity, the government drafted "Operation Campus," a joint police-military operation designed to "restore order" on Mohawk reserves and crack down on smuggling. The controversial plan called for members of JTF2 to guard water treatment plants and highways should there be a widespread rebellion as a result of the operation.

Operation Campus never saw the light of day. Days before the operation was scheduled to commence, two Québec daily newspapers broke the story. The government backed away from the action and dispersed the troops assembled in Québec. JTF2, however, was still sent into the field, to set up reconnaissance positions along known smuggling routes and feed information back to the RCMP.

Although JTF2 was off to a slow start, the Canadian government was still putting a substantial amount of resources into the unit. Even though the government announced plans to gradually reduce CF troop numbers to 52,000 from 60,000, it also expanded both the size and the mandate of JTF2. Besides counter-terrorism, the commando unit was now officially told to train for "green ops."

To meet their broadened mandate, JTF2 looked for chances to test its soldiers in real-world situations. It found that proving ground in the former Yugoslavia. The Baltic nation, which had proudly hosted the 1984 Winter Olympics, had since descended into a bloody ethnic civil war. Bosnian Serbs, supported by Serbian president Slobodan Milosevic, began moving into Serb-dominated areas of Croatia and Bosnia and Herzegovina, engaging in campaigns of ethnic cleansing against Muslims and displacing millions of refugees. Sarajevo had been reduced to a killing field as snipers from all sides opened fire on one another. Serbian troops and Bosnian Serbs executed the male populations of whole villages, raping the women and reducing buildings and homes to rubble.

The United Nations had been trying to intervene in the conflict, deploying peacekeepers from several nations, including Canada, to outposts throughout Bosnia and Herzegovina. Without the knowledge of the UN, several JTF2 bricks were also inserted into the field, practicing their reconnaissance and sniper skills in the hills and forests of the war-torn province. On more than one occasion, when regular Canadian troops were under fire, two-man teams from JTF2 slipped into the surrounding countryside to hunt for enemy snipers.

Working in Bosnia, however, proved dangerous for all members of the UN peacekeeping force. Soldiers wearing the blue beret of the UN were restricted in the use of their weapons by their peacekeeping mandate and made easy targets for Bosnian Serbs. The peril faced by UN troops was driven home in November 1994, when 400 UN Soldiers, including 55 members of the CF, were surrounded and taken hostage by Bosnian Serb troops. The move was a direct reprisal for NATO air strikes a few days earlier, to expel invading Bosnian Serbs from the UN safe zone in Bihac.

At first, the media scrambled to report the hostage-taking, but they soon began to question the seriousness of the soldiers' predicament. The hostages passed the time playing board games and talking with their "captors." Some were allowed to keep their weapons while others were simply asked to lock them away for the time being. The Serbs did nothing to harm their prisoners; they simply wouldn't allow them to leave. But the underlying threat was clear: if the UN bombing resumed, there would be casualties.

In Canada, the CF defence staff took the matter seriously. As the UN began high-level negotiations with the Serbs in an effort to secure the release of the prisoners, the Canadian government was already moving its assets into position to launch a fully armed rescue mission. JTF2 was chosen to lead the assault.

The plan, dubbed "Operation Freedom 55," was straightforward but risky. Canadian commandos, supported by U.S. Special Forces and the armoured personnel carriers (APCs) of the Royal Dragoons, would attack the compounds. If JTF2 soldiers met heavy resistance, the Dragoons would provide direct support. The problem, some Dragoon officers pointed out, was the exposure of the unit's APCs to heavy enemy fire. At Ilijas, where one group of Canadians was being held, the UN observation post was accessible only by way of a single dirt road. This left the APCs open to ambush.

Just as Operation Freedom 55 was preparing to launch, word came from Ottawa to stand down. Negotiations between the UN and Bosnian Serbs had borne fruit, and on December 8, all of the hostages were freed.

Over the next two years, Canada's crack commandos continued to train at Dwyer Hill and to undertake practical missions, but the nature of those missions began to shift. The CF began deploying JTF2 commandos as bodyguards for Canadian and foreign dignitaries. When the prime minister's nephew, Raymond Chrétien, visited Zaire during a November 1996 refugee crisis, heavily armed soldiers in reflective sunglasses stood at his elbows. JTF2 commandos also provided security for Canadian Lieutenant-General Maurice Baril when he was sent to Zaire to assess the need for UN intervention in the crisis. Photos featuring the bodyguards were accidentally released to the media, and were later reissued with the soldiers' faces blacked out or blurred.

JTF2 also began expanding its international reputation by offering security consultations and training for police forces in other countries. In 1996, a team of JTF2 operators travelled to Haiti to advise the security contingent protecting President Rene Preval from revolutionary forces. The soldiers also trained Haitian SWAT teams in raid and assault tactics to help stamp out gun smugglers in the capital of Port-au-Prince.

The unit's reputation was beginning to grow throughout the international special forces community. JTF2 soldiers were sent on exchanges to train with members of the British SAS and American Delta Force, and members of those forces were in turn sent to Dwyer Hill. JTF2 was quickly adding to the reputation of the CF as one of the world's most professional, highly trained armed forces. So it came as no surprise when JTF2 was called in to help deal with a hostage situation in Peru in 1996.

Members of the Tupac Amaru Revolutionary Army had attacked the Japanese Embassy in Lima, the capital of Peru, during an embassy function on December 17, 1996. The rebels quickly released 180 of the 380 hostages, including Canadian Ambassador Tony Vincent, but accounts from those inside suggested that the hostage-takers were prepared for a long standoff. SAS troops arrived on the scene along with a small contingent from JTF2.

As negotiations dragged on over the next few months, JTF2 officials began assembling a plan to remove the terrorists from the embassy. The operation, however, was dicey and underhanded. JTF2 operators would ambush the terrorists when and if they tried to leave the embassy to board an aircraft that would carry them to safety. The ministry of Foreign Affairs refused to sign off on the plan, and the Peruvian government declined all offers of international assistance. On April 22, 1997, a team of 140 Peruvian commandos burst into the embassy, killing all of the hostage-takers. All of the hostages were rescued, save one who suffered a heart attack during the raid.

Although JTF2 was not involved in the raid, defence staff remained convinced of the unit's importance and lobbied the government to expand it further. In 1997, the government increased the unit's size from 130 to approximately 300 soldiers and increased its budget by several million dollars. Additional support staff was assigned exclusively to the unit, including weapons technicians, medics, clerks and divers.

Over the next four years, the unit continued to increase its international profile and to provide Close Personal Protection (CPP) to Canadian dignitaries. In 1998, JTF2 soldiers accompanied former Canadian General Roméo Dallaire to Tanzania where he testified against a member of the Rwandan government accused in the genocide campaign of 1994 and 1995. JTF2 also accompanied UN Chief War Crimes Prosecutor and future Supreme Court of Canada Justice Louise Arbour to Kosovo when she toured the region during the civil war between the Serbian government and the Kosovo Liberation Army (KLA).

It was not the first time JTF2 had been linked to the ongoing conflict in the Albanian-dominated province of Kosovo. In 1999, NATO decided to launch a series of attacks against Serbian forces in Kosovo in response to widespread reports of war atrocities and ethnic cleansing. U.S. and British special forces were inserted into the countryside, identifying targets of opportunity as well as "painting" targets with ground-based laser units to guide incoming combat aircraft. Rumours emerged that members of JTF2 were involved in similar missions behind enemy lines in Kosovo, but the government, adhering to its policy of secrecy concerning the activities of JTF2, refused to confirm or deny the reports.

Thus far, JTF2's operations had been piecemeal and mostly supportive. But the tragic attacks on September 11, 2001 signalled a new beginning for the elite unit. The U.S. government quickly linked the terrorist attacks to Al-Qaeda, a terrorist group operating out of Afghanistan. Osama Bin Laden, the elusive terrorist mastermind and financier had already claimed responsibility for a series of attacks against U.S. embassies in Africa in 1998, as well as a bombing attack against a U.S. warship in 2000. That government targeted not only Bin Laden and Al-Qaeda for destruction, but also Bin Laden's Afghani hosts, the Taliban.

The Muslim ruling elite of Afghanistan had long drawn the world's ire for its treatment of women, its harsh interpretation of Muslim law and its destruction of precious archaeological artifacts. With thousands of American citizens now dead because of Al-Qaeda's attacks, President George W. Bush quickly marked the Taliban as an enemy of the United States. Within a day of the attacks, U.S. Special Forces were on the ground in Afghanistan, gathering intelligence and making contact with members of the Northern

Alliance, a rebel group engaged in a bloody civil war against the Taliban.

On October 8, Defence Minister Art Eggleton announced that six Canadian warships would be sent to Afghanistan to augment U.S. and allied forces. In a brief statement, Eggleton also stunned the press when he revealed that members of JTF2 had also been assigned to the campaign, at the request of the U.S. government. It was the first time the government had ever announced an overseas deployment of the unit.

Despite the prompt announcement, the 40-man team assigned to the international special forces (codenamed "Task Force K-Bar") did not arrive in Afghanistan until December. JTF2 was forced to rely on its American allies for insertion into the hills of Afghanistan because Canada lacked any long-range helicopters for that purpose. Once in the field, however, JTF2 threw itself into its mission. This was the first true battle test for the eight-year old unit, and the soldiers were eager to prove themselves alongside their American and British counterparts.

But the members of JTF2 and the Canadian government soon found themselves embroiled in a political firestorm. An Associated Press photographer released a photo showing Canadian commandos escorting Taliban prisoners from the back of a helicopter. Why, asked opposition MPs, had the defence minister not informed the prime minister that JTF2 troops had captured prisoners until well after the mission had been executed? This oversight almost cost the minister a Parliamentary censure for misleading the governing body.

That event gave rise to a second, more controversial issue. The U.S. government had already declared that they would treat Taliban and Al-Qaeda prisoners as "battlefield detainees" and not prisoners of war, thereby circumventing any rights they might have under the Geneva Convention. Some opposition MPs argued that this was a blatant violation of international law, and that it would therefore be wrong to hand any Canadian-captured prisoners over to the Americans.

Despite the furore on Parliament Hill, JTF2 troops continued to distinguish themselves in the battlefield in Afghanistan. In March 2002, the U.S. launched Operation Anaconda against Taliban and Al-Qaeda forces cloistered in the Shah-e-Khot Valley, south of Kabul. Two hundred members of Task Force K-BAR supported U.S. and Afghan regular troops as they drove out what was believed to be the bulk of the remaining Taliban and Al-Qaeda soldiers.

JTF2 excelled in its role with Operation Anaconda. Approximately 25 crack Canadian troops scaled mountains, up to 3000 metres high, to establish observation posts overseeing the battlefield. Wearing white smocks over their forest green camouflage, the commandos subsisted for weeks at a time in $-20°$ weather as they relayed intelligence to the regular Anaconda forces. The remaining JTF2 commandos continued patrolling the vast Afghani wilderness, helping U.S. Navy SEALS search elaborate cave networks for enemy weapons caches and intelligence.

The unit's professionalism, training and ability impressed the rest of the special forces community. SAS, SEAL and Delta Force soldiers, in offhand conversations, praised members of JTF2 for their assistance.

Two years later, in December 2004, President George W. Bush awarded JTF2 the Presidential Unit Citation. Although no details were released, the unit was selected because it "captured personnel, equipment and material of significant intelligence value and hampered the enemy's ability to conduct operations against…coalition partners."

The future of the unit appears promising. With increased government support and funding, JTF2 should continue to provide useful service in missions around the world. When the U.S. solicited assistance for its invasion of Iraq in 2003, they asked if JTF2 would be available. Though Prime Minister Chrétien refused to send Canadian troops to serve in Iraq, the U.S. government request speaks volumes for JTF2's reputation in the international community.

People within JTF2 and the CF would like to see the unit's funding and capabilities expanded further, to create a larger force that can be rapidly and covertly deployed overseas. Meanwhile, critics at home continue to worry about the fact that the unit operates outside of Parliament's oversight, leaving an opening for possible misuse by the government. Members of the media also complain about lack of access to JFT2 information, in an era where British and American special forces routinely grant interviews about their missions.

JTF2 also has several materiel and equipment needs the government has yet to address. JTF2 and the CF as a whole lack a strategic airlift capability or the ability to respond to any situation anywhere in the world rapidly. CF soldiers as well as JTF2 commandos are frequently forced to rely on their allies for transport to theatres of conflict. The unit would also benefit from the purchase of medium or long-range helicopters to insert bricks into enemy territory without having to hitch lifts from U.S., British or other allied special operations units.

If JTF2 is so well respected in the international community, they argue, Canadians should be given the opportunity to celebrate the unit's accomplishments.

Nevertheless, JTF2 has already made its presence known in the world of military intelligence and should continue to make an impact in the years ahead.

Notes on Sources

Adams, Ian. *Agent of Influence: A True Story*. Toronto: Stoddard Publishing, 1999.

Andrew, Christopher and Vasili Mitrokhin. *The Mitrokhin Archive*. London: Penguin Group, 1999.

Beeby, Dean. *Cargo of Lies: The True Story of a Nazi Double Agent in Canada*. Toronto: University of Toronto Press, 1996.

Glazov, Jamie. (2001, July). A Homosexual and Naïve Canadian Ambassador to Moscow. *Front Page Mag.com*. Retrieved December 12, 2004 from www.frontpagemag.com

Heaps, Leo. *Hugh Hambleton, Spy: Thirty Years with the KGB*. Toronto: Methuen, 1983.

Hodgson, Lynn-Phillip. *Inside Camp X*. Oakville: Blake Book Distribution, 1999.

Macdonald, Bill. *The True "Intrepid:" Sir William Stephenson and the Unknown Agents*. Surrey: Timberholme, 1998.

Mount, Graeme S. *Canada's Enemies: Spies and Spying in the Peaceable Kingdom*. Toronto: Dundurn Press, 1993.

Pugiliese, David. *Canada's Secret Commands: The Unauthorized Story of Joint Task Force Two*. Ottawa: Esprit de Corps Books, 2002.

———. *Shadow Wars: Special Forces in the New Battle Against Terrorism*. Ottawa: Esprit de Corps Books, 2003.

Robbins, Ron. (2004). *Great Contemporaries: Sir William Stephenson, "Intrepid."* Retrieved Nov. 3, 2004 from www.winstonchurchill.org/i4a/pages/index.cfm?

Sanders, Richard. *Regime Change in Canada by the US.* Retrieved December 31, 2004 from www.peace.ca/regimechangeincanada.htm

Sawatsky, John. *For Services Rendered: Leslie James Bennett and the RCMP Security Service.* Toronto: Doubleday Canada, 1982.

————. *Gouzenko: The Untold Story.* Toronto: Macmillan of Canada, 1984.

Stafford, David. *Camp X.* Toronto: Lester & Orpen Dennys, 1986.

Stafford, David. *Spy Wars: Espionage and Canada from Gouzenko to Glasnost.* Toronto: Key Porter Books, 1990.

Stevenson, William. *A Man Called Intrepid.* New York: Harcourt Brace Jovanovich, 1976.

————. *Intrepid's Last Case.* New York: Willard Books, 1983.

Thomas, Rosamund. *Espionage and Secrecy: The Official Secrets Act 1911–1989 of the United Kingdom.* London: Routledge, 1991.

Canada's Joint Task Force Two. (n.d.). Retrieved December 29, 2004 from home.blarg.net/~whitet/jtf2.htm

Joint Task Force Two. (n.d.). Retrieved January 2, 2005 from www.forces.gc.ca/dcds/units/jtf2/default_e.asp

Joint Task Force Two. (n.d.). Retrieved January 2, 2005 from www.specialoperations.com

Sir William Stephenson. (n.d.). Retrieved November 23, 2004 from www.intbranch.org/steven.htm

The Gouzenko Transcripts. Ottawa: Deneau Publishers, 1982.

～✹～